BECOMING A WARRIOR

The Power of a Healed Heart

JASON HILL

Becoming a Warrior: The Power of a Healed Heart, 2ⁿᵈ Edition

Copyright © 2024 by Jason Hill

Published in 2024 by Guerote LLC & Young Warriors Foundation

Cover Design: Keira Dooley, Dooley Design Group

Book Design: Courtney Rae

Editing: Annie K. Preston, Vanessa Garcia and Jason Hill

Paperback ISBN: 979-8-9880065-2-7

Printed in the United States of America

Los Angeles, California

This book is dedicated to...

My warrior daughter, Ana.

You are my real-life superhero and my north star.

—Dad

To my beautiful and funny Mom.
Mom, life didn't make it easy for you, I understand that.
I love you. I forgive you.

To Vanessa Garcia.
The most magnificent and beautiful soul I've ever
known. My daughter became our daughter, you are a
living legend in my eyes. The world needs to know you
— you're a true gift to the universe. I love you deeply,

PRAISE FOR THE FIRST EDITION

If you enjoy reading inspirational memoirs, *Becoming a Warrior: The Power of a Healed Heart*, by Jason Hill is for you. Although written from a traditional chronological approach, this is a quintessentially human story that can inspire people of any faith, race, creed, national origin, or age to view the daily challenges in life with hopefulness, positivity, humility, and gratitude. From his traumatic entrance into this world, through boyhood in economically and socially constrained surroundings to his impressive personal redemptions and achievements in service, civic activism, and leadership, you cannot help but be inspired by Jason Hill's determination, tough-mindedness, and moral courage which are balanced by his humility, fairness, and devotion to family. A vivid and raw recollection of life-changing events, a list of truisms and words of wisdom, and a timeline that emphasizes the many redemptive episodes of his life are included. A noticeable stream is clear as he lists the people and organizations which influenced and assisted him along the way for better or for worse, thus emphasizing the point of "you are not alone" and "know and build your village."

In *Becoming a Warrior: The Power of a Healed Heart*, Jason Hill gives us an autobiography that is both edifying and hopeful. The well-paced narrative flows through the chronology of his life and is utterly engaging. I didn't want to put it down. My favorite chapter is Chapter 6: Wounded Healer, as it is within these pages where Jason Hill enters the fork in the road and chooses his Young Warrior Path. Having chosen the Young Warrior path did not guarantee anything to get easier as we later learn, yet it is the Young Warrior principles learned and adopted that guarantee a stronger foundation and consistency when facing life challenges and trauma. That message resonates with the masses and is as timely as ever, and I wish it could be plastered on the front page or virtual equivalent of every news media in the country. This is the story of an inspirational human life underpinned and strengthened by a development of deep faith in God and humanity. His story's twist is at the end as he reveals the full meaning of W.A.R.R.I.O.R.S. and advocates for its spread far and wide, which makes me wonder why it is not weaved front and center. Highly recommended.

Cesar Lopez
Executive Director, Education Nonprofit

After reading Jason's book, I gained so much admiration and respect for Jason Hill. This man has been through three lifetimes worth of trauma and his perseverance is colossal. His journey is exhilarating. His unshakable faith is encouraging and so inspirational. *Becoming a Warrior* will change and save lives.

Joumana Kidd
Journalist—Philanthropist

Jay has had a life that few can possibly imagine and very few of us would have the will and grit to not only survive but thrive as he has. His life story (so far) as chronicled in this exceptional book, is rivaled only by his unselfish dedication and commitment to those who need a guiding hand and voice to become who they can be.

John Chisholm
Managing Director, John Chisholm Group
Retired CEO, Flotek Industries

Jay Hill's *Becoming a Warrior* is an inspiring work. Actually, Jason himself is inspiring. Reading about his childhood, adolescence, and the struggles he and his mother endured and seeing the man he is today will be an encouragement to so many young men, i.e., warriors. Such a positive example as Jason tells about the willingness he had to make a transformation, the road of turning ideas and thought into actions. *Becoming a Warrior* is an excellent book and will help young men and women overcome challenges and transform to have a better future. Thank you, Jason, for sharing your story!

Anita Castille
AHF (AIDS Healthcare Foundation)

CONTENTS

FOREWORD

How about those war movie heroes in **Gladiator** or **Braveheart**? You ever wonder how in the world they are able to take on countless fights and to some degree even lose the fight, but ultimately win in the end? You see, their spirit was not crushed. In fact, they were hard pressed on every side, overthrown and even killed; but they were never separated from LOVE. You must wonder, which love is that? It is called self-love. The ability to love yourself so you can love others. It is the love that will pick up the spirit of a fellow brother. A love that will save a nation. And even a love that will resurrect the dead. A healing love that will alter the trajectory of your life and the life of others.

You see, my dear friend, Jason Hill, should have never made it out. Forget a cat with nine lives. We are talking 9,999 lives, and then some. He is an anomaly. Before he was pushed out into this world, he was already set up with disadvantages in the womb. This man is my ex-husband. Yeah, you read that right. After all these years, I shake my head in wonder and awe over how he is here today. I am proud of who he has become. It's the heart and continuous fight within him that stirs up my soul. I always seem to find myself rooting for the underdogs, the ordinary, those who are perceived with the least advantage, and when you see them rise and conquer – there is nothing like it in the world.

Yes, you will read some unfortunate tough moments, but I can assure that you will be incredibly moved and inspired by his warrior way of overcoming. It's the voice of God that whispers and calls, but it's up to the heart to respond. Oh, and you better believe he responds. When you see that much resilience, you can't help but to be moved. Regardless of whatever is going on in your life, Jason's words will speak to you in one way or another. We, too, have our own paths and journeys to travel and this book is intended for you, so read it as you. It's for everyone, but especially for those who can't seem to see the way out. Hope may be grim, and the people in your life aren't who they are supposed to be, but guess what? It is a blessing to battle this one out because you are worth fighting for. And the better news is that you will find you have had your maker in your corner all along. Fight the good fight, my friend, and be inspired by one of the greatest fighters I know. And to those that have been in the trenches already and have had some victories, well—the battles are never really over, are they? Each battle prepares you for the next great big one. You may wonder, is it worth it? A resounding YES! You are worth it! You grow stronger, wiser, and more mature; but most of all, you learn about love and your heart. Real love. God's love.

It is an honor to have been in this gentle giant man's life as long as I have. His generosity and big heart shows day in and day out. His courage and truth have created the awareness to look within myself to be set free. And free I am and there is no turning back. That is what he does. How did he do that? He's doing what? He made it through what? Huh....? Utter bewilderment, indeed. So buckle up, because you are in for an inspiring and powerful ride.

May God continue to bless and evolve you, my dear friend.

Cheers to becoming a true warrior,

Vanessa Garcia

Founder, Wellness By Vanessa G.

Co-Founder, Young Warriors

INTRODUCTION

L ife isn't fair for anyone. And there are some who have it worse than others, depending on a number of things: social status, income, color of skin, gender, and a myriad of other demographic indicators.

Throughout this book, I'll be real with you. I'll share the raw, unfiltered truths of my life – the battles I've fought, the demons I've faced, and the victories I've won. And I'll show you how to fight your own battles, face your own demons, and claim your own victories. Because this isn't just my story; it's a roadmap for your journey.

Remember, this isn't about becoming someone else. It's about becoming the best version of yourself. It's about stripping away the bullshit, the excuses, and the lies you've been telling yourself. It's about facing the man in the mirror and demanding more from him. It's about stepping into the arena, battered and bruised, but never beaten.

And yes, I talk about faith, about God, and I cuss. I do it with the same passion with which I live every aspect of my life. I pray hard, and I fight hard. My relationship with the divine is mine alone – unapologetic, raw, and real. It's part of my strength, part of my journey, and it's non-negotiable. So, if you're ready to embrace this journey with all its complexities, contradictions, and challenges, then you're in the right place.

As we embark on this journey together, remember this – you're not alone. I'm right here with you, every step of the way. Together, we'll face the storms, conquer the mountains, and emerge victorious. Because that's what warriors do. They fight, they overcome, and they inspire.

So, are you ready to become the warrior you were always meant to be? Are you ready to turn your pain into power, your struggles into strength, and your story into a legacy? If your answer is a resounding 'hell yes', then let's get to work. The path won't be easy, but I promise you, it'll be the most rewarding journey of your life. Let's go, big dog. It's time to unleash the badass, heart-led warrior within you!

Now, let's cut through the bullshit. This book isn't just a collection of words; it's a call to arms. It's a challenge to rise above the mediocrity, the excuses, and the bullshit that's been holding you back. It's about igniting that fire in your belly, that unquenchable thirst to be more, do more, and achieve more. This is where you stop being a victim of your circumstances and start being the master of your fate.

I'm not here to coddle you. I'm here to push you, to provoke you, to piss you off if that's what it takes to wake you up to your own potential. Because let's face it, the world is full of people who will tell you it's okay to be just okay. But I'm not one of those people. I'm here to tell you that 'okay' is not okay. You're not meant for mediocrity. You're meant for greatness.

Throughout this book, I'll be real with you. I'll share the raw, unfiltered truths of my life – the battles I've fought, the demons I've faced, and the victories I've won. And I'll show you how to fight your own battles, face your own demons, and claim your own victories. Because this isn't just my story; it's a roadmap for your journey.

Remember, this isn't about becoming someone else. It's about becoming the best version of yourself. It's about stripping away the bullshit, the excuses, and the lies you've been telling yourself. It's about facing the man in the mirror and demanding more from him. It's about stepping into the arena, battered and bruised, but never beaten.

And yes, I talk about faith, about God, and I do it with the same passion with which I live every aspect of my life. I pray, I cuss, I believe hard and I love hard. My relationship with the divine is mine alone – unapologetic, raw, and real. Love, It's part of my strength, part of my journey, and it's non-negotiable. So, if you're ready to embrace this journey with all its complexities, contradictions, and challenges, then you're in the right place.

As we embark on this journey together, remember this – you're not alone. I'm right here with you, every step of the way. Together, we'll face the storms, conquer the mountains, and emerge victorious. Because that's what warriors do. They fight, they overcome, and they inspire.

So, are you ready to become the warrior you were always meant to be? Are you ready to turn your pain into power, your struggles into strength, and your story into a legacy? If your answer is a resounding 'hell yes', then let's get to work. The path won't be easy, but I promise you, it'll be the most rewarding journey of your life. Let's go, big dog. It's time to unleash the badass, heart-led warrior within you.

"Who said anything about safe? 'Course he isn't safe.
But he is good."

- C.S. Lewis, Chronicles of Narnia

CHAPTER 1
ALONE IN THE WILDERNESS

L ife was a battle way before I was even born. I was being formed into a Warrior from the very beginning. My mom wasn't capable of taking care of herself, let alone a child. You see, she was a drug addict and an alcoholic. During this time, she was intimate with a man who got her pregnant. Sadly, she doesn't know who it was. Imagine that. Picture being 22 years old and getting pregnant by someone, but you don't know who. All of a sudden, you wake up one day and find out you are having a baby; about to bring a human being into this world, and you have no idea who the other half of this child belongs to. It was all too much for her and it became overwhelming to think she could do this and do it on her own. Attempting to end my life at the abortion clinic four separate times, she could never go through with it. She knew she wasn't ready to have a child, but something in her fought to try. While pregnant, she grew to love me as I grew in her belly.

I was born on July 1, 1975, in Columbus, Ohio. It was a traumatic birth, with my mother and me both spending the first few weeks in the ICU (intensive care unit). There were some complications related to her drug use, so they had to keep us there for observation.

To this day, I don't know who my biological father is. I have no information about him. Sadly, I don't know his name, ethnicity, character traits, looks, thoughts, feelings... *nothing*. We really had little information to go on. Unless a miracle happens, I will most likely never know who the man is, because my mother doesn't know. We had no starting point. I first became conscious of this in elementary school. I felt ashamed and embarrassed that I didn't have a dad.

Mom's sister, Aunt Gayle, and Uncle Ken took me in for about 6-8 months when I was around eighteen months old. She cared for my well-being and loved me, and at the end of the day wanted to make sure I was all right. She knew what was going on with her sister and did what was in her heart to do. However, I ended up going back to live with my mom.

My mom was in another relationship five years later and gave birth to my precious baby sister, Amanda. Mom's unhealthy patterns didn't change. I knew she loved Amanda and me, but that love didn't always show up in her words or actions. She was far too broken to make the best decisions for herself or our family. She was conflicted about her lifestyle, and that inner struggle led to emotional tsunamis. One minute she'd be screaming at my sister or me at the top of her lungs; then two minutes later, she'd be sobbing on the floor, apologizing profusely, and telling us how much she loved us. Her emotions simply flowed out without a filter or a throttle. If she was happy, everyone was happy; but when she was angry or depressed, my sister and I suffered with her. So many ups and downs, we didn't know what to expect. Things never felt safe or stable.

Family picture: Jason (left), Mom Denise (center), Sister Amanda (right)

I will say, however, I enjoyed having my sister's dad, Don, around. He cared for me like a father for the few years he was with my mom. Of course, I knew he was my sister's dad, and not really my dad. I kind of felt like I was a burden, but I don't think he thought that at all. When we got together with his family, I never felt like I fit. There were signs that felt like they barely tolerated me, especially his mom, my sister's grandmother. I could deal with that because I knew when we got home, Don would be caring and loving toward me; he never did anything to make me feel like I wasn't really his son. But like most of my mother's relationships, theirs was short-lived due to hardcore drug use and character issues. And just to think, things would get even worse.

Ever since I can remember, I craved my mother's love and her presence. I was a mama's boy for sure. I desired to be held and loved by her. I worried about her when she didn't show up for days. And when she returned, she would be so drunk or high, I couldn't even talk to her. I was afraid for her and would lay next to her, hoping nothing bad would happen. One morning is etched in my brain forever. I was waiting for her to come home. She was on pills and something else. I said, "Mommy, I'm hungry." I must have been about 6 years old. She was wobbling all over the kitchen, holding onto whatever was near her and mumbling incoherently the entire time. She grabbed a tomato and put it in the microwave. It exploded and we both jumped back. It scared us and I was shocked and felt weird inside, like we were in trouble. Then she got the orange juice out of the refrigerator and kept pouring it in the glass on the counter until it overflowed. I watched her keep pouring and pouring the juice as it ran out the glass. I was scared for her.

I used to see all kinds of weird paraphernalia around her room. Her friends talked openly about using drugs. I already knew she was popping pills and drinking excessively, but I didn't know about the crystal meth. There were always men of various sizes and drunkenness floating in and out of our lives. Our house was a place for excessive drinking and drug use. I lived in that type of environment for the next two decades of my life. My mom would leave me home alone or with babysitters, anyone really, for weeks at a time. There was a time she left me at a drug addict's house; a male stranger she didn't even know. for about ten days straight. You can only imagine the things that went on. It was a devastating start for a young boy's life. I started shutting down. I would go to my room and lay on my bed and be in there afraid and alone for hours talking to my finger. I would turn my finger toward me and wiggle it up and down, imagining it was talking back. I would also have conversations with my Kermit the Frog doll. They were like my confidantes. I felt like I was actually talking to them. You know how kids' imaginations are. It was my safe place. I know it may sound weird, but honestly, "Kermie" and my finger were my trusted friends, and they were all I had.

Immediately after that, I developed a chronic neurological motor tic in my cervical neck area, which would cause my head to twitch forward under stressful situations. This is something that often affects children who are dealing with tremendous stress or trauma. It is the body's way of processing for the child who is in an extremely unstable or traumatic environment. I needed to feel in control and that control turned into compulsive responses. Unfortunately, we were never able to deal with this properly as a kid because when I was in second grade, the doctors misdiagnosed me with a neurological condition called Tourette's Syndrome, as well as ADHD and OCD, among other diagnoses. They prescribed Haldol. Haldol (haloperidol) is a psychotic drug that treats disorders like schizophrenia, helps control Tourette's, and is used to treat severe behavior problems in children. I did have several behavioral issues, but what I really needed was to be loved and protected. One of the side effects is feeling sleepy. It basically acted like a sedative; it would knock me out and make me sleep in most of my classes, and when I was up, I was a zombie. I wasn't learning and there sure wasn't anyone holding me accountable at home.

I didn't want to be home, but it wasn't any safer at school because I was always being called out, pointed at, and made fun of by my peers. Kids can be cruel. So, what did I do? I turned things around and made it work for me. Well, so I thought. When the twitch came on, of course, I was being stared and laughed at. I didn't know how to cope with what was happening because I didn't know what was happening myself, I was just a young hurting boy. I was embarrassed and because I was already silly anyway, I exaggerated it. That way, people couldn't see who I really was. They were laughing AT me. So, I joined in. I thought, why not have them laugh with me? I didn't want to be left alone and excluded. I can't believe I joined in on the bullying of myself. I had introduced myself to another level of trauma as a kid, and I didn't know what the hell was going on. I just knew I liked to see people laugh and I liked to laugh... to me that meant happiness. It meant relief. It meant I got to keep some of my friends. I guess that's what I wanted deep down inside. This was the first time I learned to perform and hide behind an act so no one could really see the pain underneath it all.

Actually, a lot of comedians do this with their pain as grown adults. And this twitch that they just so happened to misdiagnose as Tourette's Syndrome at the time... no one understood it. I didn't understand it. My mom didn't understand it. My teachers didn't understand it. They would leave me alone and let me sleep because they had the doctor's note that indicated what the medication would do to me. And to think this was my first real drug use. I was eight years old. Un-freakin'-believable. Now, what I could've used was a big ass hug and protection from a strong caring male figure inviting me into his arms, holding me and telling me with love that I don't have to do all that... and that I was awesome. I would want him to tell me that I was amazing, whole, and that nothing was wrong with me. Unfortunately, most times when a man was around, I was disrespected, pushed aside and abused, both verbally and physically. And it was horrible. There were no male role models. Sad to say, because of this, I ended up carrying heavy shame for most of my childhood and into adulthood.

Most kids have their father or another adult male to teach and guide them through the process of life. Like learning to ride their first bike—I had no one. I remember learning with a bunch of kids in the housing projects when we lived in Columbus. I was scared as hell at first. That's how life is: sometimes we have the help, and sometimes we don't. When we don't, it's more tempting to quit before ever trying. You may not be able to keep the bike steady at first. You could fall off and scrape your knees, but that's part of learning new things. That's all part of the process. But if you let your fear of falling stop you, you'll never learn to ride the damn bike!

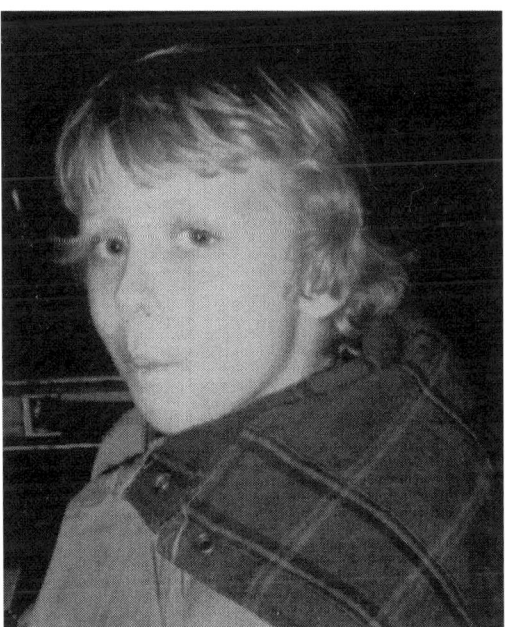

Jason, Columbus Ohio. Eight years old

Mom needed help with Amanda and me, so we moved to Akron to be closer to my grandma. This was in the early 80s. The extra hand was needed now that Mom had two children. Akron, Ohio, in the early 80s was a rough city, with a mixture of Black and White residents. We lived in the Section 8 projects in Eastland Woods (Section 8 projects are government subsidized low-income housing projects). All residents lived in poverty: about 80% were Black, and the rest of us were White.

Grandma Ruth, who also lived in Section 8 housing her entire life, she was something else. Tough as nails but with a big heart for me. She was my safe place when Mom was in jail. But it wasn't just her in my life. Aunt Terry, she had her own battles too. Her life was rough, tangled up in the world of the streets and prostitution. She lost her kids to Child Services because of her drug problems, and that hurt never left her.

I remember this one time with Aunt Terry, clear as day in my mind. We were in a car, driven by a man I knew at the time only as Doug, a cool guy. Only later did I come to realize that he was her pimp. He was driving, not her. I was just a kid, sitting in the backseat without a seatbelt, oblivious to the full reality of the situation. They were both drinking and whatever else. And man, did things go south fast. We got into a car crash. The car smashed into the back of another, and I flew forward like a baseball from a bat. Scared the crap out of me.

But, something crazy happened. Her pimp, this big guy who was definitely no hero, did something heroic. As I was flying towards the windshield, he reached out with his arm and blocked me from hitting the glass. His forearm hit my head, knocking me back. It hurt, sure, but it probably saved my life. It's one of those things, you know, that shows how wild it was back then.

That's the kind of stuff I lived through. It wasn't all bad though.

Like Grandma Ruth, she could be real sweet too. Always had a hot meal for me, and man, could she bake cookies! I still love those cookies. And watching football with her, that's how I became a die-hard Browns fan.

But Mom, she had it rough growing up in all that mess. She never learned to love herself, you know? She's amazing, but she doesn't see it. When she wasn't in jail, it was like walking on eggshells in the morning. Hangovers, withdrawal, always angry. I remember this one time, she yelled out at the top of her lungs...

"Who ate my fucking muffins?!"

She got nicer as the day wore on, and then, by nighttime, she would disappear. My baby sister and I had an intensely tough upbringing based on our mother's complete lack of personal responsibility. She had a horrible childhood herself, but she was doing the best she could with the few tools she had been given. Those tools just weren't enough to give me and my baby sister what we needed. I know our mom loved us the best way she knew how, but the sad reality was that her drug addiction and the men in her life took priority over herself and her children. We were not safe.

Mom was also being abused, both physically and mentally. Her lack of responsibility was very damaging to us. We often experienced verbal and physical abuse, as well. One time she brought in a man who was 6'5" and 280 lbs. That man wore a size fifteen shoe and had long hair and a full black beard. He rode a Harley Davidson, wore leather boots and a biker jacket. His motorcycle club did some shady business. (Similar to the Hells Angels Motorcycle Gang.) He did drugs and was drunk all the time. For the most part they depended on food stamps, but there were times when they did have jobs, Mostly, my mom was the one who worked. For the times they didn't work, they would depend on the government to pay and feed them and us. We were on welfare and the government delivered milk and cheese to our porch every week. The home was full of arguments and abuse. Late one night I heard some yelling, which was normal, but this one was a little more intense. The fight went beyond being physical and my mom pulled out his shotgun and he ended up grabbing it, then hitting her with it. I saw my mom's bloody face. I remember screaming, crying, and running back up to my room and hiding under my bed. At the time, I could not verbalize what was happening. This was some serious trauma.

Growing up the child of an addicted mother and no father figure took quite a toll on me. I emulated the bad influences around me, those very flawed adult men who drifted in and out of my life, based on my mother's whims. I picked up terrible habits from my mom and her friends' behaviors.

There were always cans of Busch Beer in the fridge, and I knew that if I took one or two no one would notice because there were always too many to count. I took my first drink in the 4th or 5th grade and that became a regular habit for me. My baby sister and I learned from our mom's example of no self-control. Amanda could never really tame her tongue. There would be fighting matches all the time with Mom, and in the event our mom brought home a stranger and if any man said anything to my baby sister, she would fire back. She didn't care and, unlike me, she wasn't afraid.

I didn't have any examples of people taking personal responsibility in my life up to that point. I would spend my summers at Don's house, my sister's biological father. I view him as a father – to this day. Don and his wife at the time, Anita, took care of me as if I were their child, too. They had a beautiful boy named Travis who I consider my brother. Travis is one of the strongest and kindest souls you will ever meet. Don had a great trucking career and Anita was making good money working for the government. Sadly, they got into drugs, and it became pretty heavy. I remember seeing huge black garbage bags everywhere full of marijuana. Plates full of cocaine were in their room. There were always people over doing drugs while Travis, Amanda, and I were hanging out. One day, Don was pulled over and the cops found 14 grams of cocaine on him, so he served time in prison. He lost his trucker's license, and his career was over. During his time in prison, Anita was spiraling out of control and downhill fast. She ended up having an affair with Don's oldest son. This was Don's son from another woman. Little Travis was eight years old, as he watched his older half-brother come over and cozy up to his mom. He was ten years older than me. I looked up to him and thought he was super cool. I must have been in the 6th grade when he taught me how to sniff random things like glue, paint thinner, or whatever substance could get us high. We would sneak out of the house, and he would take me on joy rides, and every now and then he would make pit stops to steal or buy drugs. He stole a bunch of shotguns once and ended up committing first degree armed robbery. After spending 15 years in prison, and only out just a few months, he was sentenced to another 25 years. Years later, Anita was caught in the middle of a bad drug deal. She was shot in the head and killed in the middle of her mother's driveway. It was devastating, especially for my little stepbrother, Travis.

We moved back and forth between Columbus, Akron, and Cuyahoga Falls, so I would have to jump from school to school in the elementary grades, then to high school. I never felt truly settled. In 6th grade, in Cuyahoga Falls, the basketball team had tryouts, and I didn't know what I was doing. I was the only boy who didn't make the team. I didn't know the fundamentals or have any guidance. I was lost and didn't have a man in my life to teach me sports or regular boy stuff. I didn't understand the rules, so the only one who didn't make the team was me. I was so embarrassed. I could never really make long-standing friends with anyone until we were in Akron because we kept moving from one place to another. I hadn't even hit puberty yet and friends were putting pressure on me to do it with a girl, and I knew I wasn't ready for that. I had no idea what to do or what I was doing. There we were at a church, under a bus, on the cold pavement. It was a horrible and negative experience. A rumor got out saying I didn't know what I was doing because, to be honest, I didn't know what I was doing. And it messed me up. Teens are cruel sometimes; everyone knows that. Sadly, later in life I bought into the narrative that I didn't know what I was doing or that I wasn't good at it, which later translated to a belief system of mine that I wasn't man enough. So, I was determined to prove this self-talk wrong once I hit puberty in high school. I'd have sex with nearly every girl I met just to prove to myself and others that I was a real man who could please a woman. I was determined to change the negative narrative about me as a man even though I was still just a boy. Sex became a god and a source of confidence. I really needed a male figure in my life. I really needed my dad or a positive male to protect me from others and from myself. This is where I started to take care of my ego and began to unconsciously destroy myself thinking that the destructive things I was doing were good things. I sometimes wonder what I could have been, had my dad been in my life to love, guide, and inspire me.

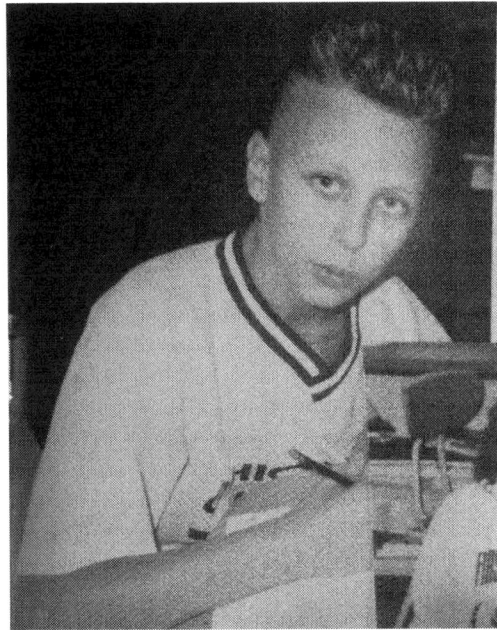

Jason high school 9th grade

I remember when I was in junior high at a high school football game under the bleachers tossing the football around and chasing some friends. I easily chased down one of the football players and noticed that one of the high school coaches saw me. He was smiling and all I kept wondering was if he noticed how fast I ran. I needed to be affirmed, believed in, and guided.

When we moved to Akron, it felt nice to feel some sort of kinship. Many of the people in our neighborhood were minorities, mostly Black, and that was the culture I grew up in while living there. I always felt accepted and loved by them. My Black neighbors fed me and laughed *with* me, not *at* me.

My best friend at the time, Wayne, and his mom would often have me over to eat dinner and stay the night. They had an inviting spirit. She was also a single mom, with a very clean and comfortable house environment.

I didn't see her partying or see different men coming in and out of her home. You could hear the fried chicken sizzling and smell it from that first knock at the door. Every time I came in, she would be playing... *Casanova* by LeVert and similar R&B soul-filled music. We were only neighbors for a few years, but it made a lasting impression on me. In my case, I found my mom passed out on a regular basis and had to eat food quickly before the men she dated would come over and eat everything. Wayne's mom was so kind to me. Wayne and I went to the same junior high school. He was fun and outgoing, and a good friend. I never felt like Wayne looked at me as a White person or any different from him. I felt like his friend, and I was always included.

Miserably, we had to move yet again. Even though we lived in the most terrible neighborhoods in Columbus and Akron, Cuyahoga Falls was the worst experience for me. I started attending school there and felt like I never fit in. I was always defending myself. I was small, poor, and very insecure and I didn't have cool clothes. I remember once a girl asked me, "Why do you always wear the same jeans?"

The truth was, I did wear the same jeans, but I lied to her, saying I had many pairs that looked the same. I was too urban in the way I talked and the way I dressed to fit in at this school. I wore my MC Hammer pants, rocked a fade, and had shaved lines in my eyebrows. I also loved hip-hop culture. Wu-Tang, NWA, MC Eiht, LL Cool J, 2Pac and Gang Starr were my favorite rappers. They articulated and used their voices in a way that I could identify with. It was pretty cool how some people could use their voice in such methodically genius ways. It spoke to me because they rapped about where they came from, and that they were not in that place anymore. They were somewhere better and wherever that was, that just sounded great to me. I wanted to be somewhere better, too.

I was considered the ultimate White trash living in a dirty, drug-filled house with motorcycles and grease all over my driveway. The cops knew who we were, especially who I was. The neighbors didn't like us. Even though these artists were a source of inspiration, the reality, though, is that I'm blue-eyed with blond hair and have white skin. I know with that comes privilege. But to be real, I couldn't make those connections back then in my young mind. All I know is that I was being fed positivity from passionate, experienced creators. I needed that to get me through. As a boy, I felt alienated from my place there in Cuyahoga Falls and the ironic thing is, it was from those with the same color skin as me that I mostly felt rejected. I was really confused. It should feel like home to all of us no matter where we step, where we come from, or how we speak. The injustices, sadly, of this nation have proved wrong and kids like me have become outsiders, looked down upon, especially as juveniles. We are not taken seriously, or even seen as a human being with any value to offer. They are often dismissed as a loss. We can become hurt by the ignorance, hate, and inadequacies of the adults or environments that we find ourselves in. And I am a man with white skin. Imagine what it is like for those of color. Hip-hop just had a precise language that I understood.

Eminem came out after I was out of high school. Sometimes people would compare me to him. His influence made it okay for other White boys to emulate what I had already been doing. He, too, had a turbulent upbringing. He gave a cool and positive face for me and the rest of us who loved hip-hop culture. Perhaps some of the upper preppy White classes developed a sense of compassion and relatability. Who knows? Whatever it was, it was refreshing to see. But I ask you, wouldn't it have been nice to maybe have had that in my high school days? I was called Eminem in my mid-twenties. In fact, some people even mistook me for him in Los Angeles. My hair was just like his. One night in L.A. I went to the Century Club, which was a hot spot in the 90's. Some random guy kind of nervous-like walked up to me and asked, "Are you Eminem?" I could tell how excited he was with his CD in his hand, and hoping I was, in fact, Eminem. For that split second, I blurted out, "Yeah." To be honest, I didn't want to disappoint him at that moment, I wanted to ride the wave of feeling like a star. I wanted to feel respected, admired, and valued. He started to tell me about his own music and how good it was. Handing me his CD, he asked me to listen to it. Standing across from us was the rapper, Warren G. I could tell he was listening to me talk and probably thinking... "This little lying ass punk..." Looking back, I can't believe myself sometimes. Freaking hilarious.

I knew I was different, and so were a group of us poor White boys who couldn't afford preppy clothes. So, we became the misfits, aka "White Trash." One of the guys in the group was David Hite, who became another one of my best friends. When I say we came from the same side of the tracks, boy, let me tell you. He, too, was a White kid living in Section 8 with no father in the home; and his mom was just like mine. We clicked right away. He was a short guy, and he was hella crazy. Once he got into a fist fight with a tree. He was always angry and depressed, but funny and charismatic. Dave always had a way with the ladies. We both understood each other because we had the same background, but we were very much misunderstood by the rest of the kids at school.

Like, hey—you're not one of us, and you certainly ain't no Black kid either. Man, I was just being me, and that was not ok, so I subconsciously learned to people-please at an early age to protect the outside world from disliking me for who I really was. It was like a game instead of "hide and seek;" let's call it "hide and please."

But high school wasn't that bad. I made two other life-long friends there, despite feeling out of place. Two White guys, both named Michael that, to this day, honor their titles as hillbillies. I can say that because I know it to be true. Back then – I had that hillbilly in me. Probably still do, deep down inside.

Man, how I longed for the times when we lived in Akron or Columbus, because there I felt accepted and liked by the other kids. Even the White kids were more like me. I am a White man, however, my spirit, soul, and especially my heart, have been shaped and nurtured in a multicultural way. But to understand me and my personality, you must first understand my childhood. My mom fed me and kept me alive and did the best she could considering her childhood and addictions. I knew she loved me in the best way she knew how. But let's just face it; it wasn't near enough and it was never safe. My mom did what she knew. I experienced neglect and abuse. I never met my father. All her boyfriends were White biker types and at the time, either verbally or physically abused me—constantly, and daily, including her present husband.

Follow me on this.

When we moved to an all-White area, in Cuyahoga Falls, I just didn't feel accepted by most of the kids at school. I was bullied by all the preppy White kids. I tried to be like them for years because even though my skin was White, I kept feeling that I wasn't among them. It reminds me of the story of Mowgli in *The Jungle Book* by Rudyard Kipling. I mentioned it earlier, and now I want to expand on what I was thinking. As a baby, he was left in the jungle with all the other animals. The beautiful mighty wolves raised him with so much love. He walked on all four limbs like them, ate like them, and even talked like them. However, even among them were those who criticized him because he didn't look like them. By the time he made it to a village with humans on it, they thought he was an outcast and a threat and even put him in a cage. Regardless of which side he was with, he was judged and criticized for not being one of them. Once taken out of one world, he learns to now adjust to another, but never really understanding his own. He felt a conflict deep within him between the jungle and the village. He had an inherent innocence, searching for identity. In the *Mowgli* movie, he quotes, *"I am not a wolf. I am not a man. I am Mowgli. Mowgli, man and wolf. Both and neither."* The one thing he could identify himself with was his heart. He was a warrior and fought to give a voice to the voiceless and a face to the faceless, even though he was perceived as a misfit in both worlds. Misunderstood. He brought nature and man together and took responsibility for his community. This goes to show that we are products of our environment, but more than that, we are human beings with a soul and heart.

Why couldn't I be myself and be accepted as I was? It was confusing and hurtful. I was a kid and didn't know any other way to be. I tried to fit in, though. I did. I tried to be a country boy, a raver, then a rocker type, which they called "burn-outs." I even grew a mullet. I tried being preppy too, but that was hard because I was poor, and everyone knew it. The preppy kids were wearing brands like Polo, Ralph Lauren, and penny loafers, and I couldn't afford any of that. I would at times go to the nice department stores, head into the fitting rooms, and put on the new brand-named clothes and leave my old garments behind. I would then just walk right out of the store. When I was myself, they called me a "wigger," which means a White guy who wants to be a Black guy. How is that? I wasn't trying to be anything but myself. I dressed and acted like all my other friends, so what was the difference? I just didn't get it at the time. Dave and I were called wiggers and bullied for real. Just because we didn't act "White." What does that even mean? Well, we know exactly what that means, and it is wrong on all levels. I was jumped a few times and they busted my lip. My school locker was broken into, and they stole all my stuff. They knocked books out of my hands in the hallway, and so many more mean things like that. I felt like a joke to them.

I experienced all kinds of judgment, racism, and hate, and not just at school. I came home with corn rows and John, my mom's now-husband, would call me a fucking Nigger. That's right with a hard N and ending with an E-R. The man was terrifying. Basically, he called me that whenever he was frustrated with me. It has to be the most offensive word out there. His ignorance was overwhelming. One evening I was home on the phone, and he called on the other line from a bar looking for my mom.

He said, "Go get your mom."

Then I said, "She isn't here, bye."

Fifteen minutes later, I heard footsteps rushing up the stairs. While I was still on the phone, he started wailing on me and yelling, "Don't you ever fucking hang up on me again!" He punched me in the face and busted my nose. Blood was everywhere, including on my bed sheets.

Then he yelled, "Clean this fucking shit up, and you better not tell your mother!"

I was so afraid. I couldn't move. Another time, he threw a Ragu spaghetti sauce glass jar across the room that broke over my shoulder and the sauce splattered all over me. I felt worthless in his presence. There were so many despicable men who shaped me to believe my entire childhood that men with my same color of skin disliked me because early on, most of them who were in my life on a regular basis treated me like I was worthless.

I sat down on the cold concrete floor in the basement and cried to my mom, asking her to stop drinking and using drugs. I also begged her to leave him. My mom cried and said she would do that if I really wanted her to, but it was like she was putting it all on me.

I remember telling her, "I want you to leave him. I hate him, but it's up to you. If you don't want to, I understand. I know that you love him."

Long story short, she married that man and is still with that man today.

I remember feeling like I genuinely wanted to hurt this man. Have you ever heard the term, hurt people, hurt people? I thought about how to plot his death and I thought about it often. All the abuse and pain he caused on my family was overwhelming. I played the scenario in my head. I could call my friends over and wait for him to come through the door one day and we could jump him, and I could take my fist to him over and over again. I could beat him with all the pain and suffering that was in me. Of course, I never touched him, but boy did I really think about it. If there would have been an opportunity, I would've taken it. I never told anyone what was going on in my head, but it was as real as it gets.

There have been times when my life was such a struggle and I wished my mom would have terminated her pregnancy or put me up for adoption. There were also times when it seemed the world and I were not meant for each other. I wanted to quit but didn't. I often thought to myself, "There has to be a reason why I was born."

Violence was everywhere. One kid stabbed another kid with a pencil over breakfast tickets. The environment I grew up in was unhealthy and tragic—and full of death. One friend shot himself in the head over a heartbreak, another one fell off a cliff while on drugs, and two overdosed at a concert. At this point, I was drinking a 12-pack of beer with friends at 6 a.m. in the park and smoking weed right before class. I was 15 years old, and I was feeling angry and frustrated all the time.

I had a girlfriend when I was still in high school. Zoe was my first true love, and I loved her deeply, but I had never witnessed or been taught by anyone on how to be a respectful, loving, and caring man. I had only seen how the men my mom brought around behaved, mostly yelling and hitting. Zoe meant everything to me, but that didn't stop me from cheating on her multiple times, sneaking around behind her back, and verbally attacking her. We started drinking and smoking marijuana together. Regretfully, I had moments when I was very drunk, I shoved and yelled obscenities at her. She didn't deserve any of that. Ever. I wish a man was around to teach me and show me how a woman was supposed to be treated. I didn't have an example. Realizing how much I hated being hit or seeing my mom hit, I didn't like it, but I did what I saw. I thought the verbal attacks were enough to scare someone and make a point. So I started to do it, too. At the time, I didn't understand how much it truly hurt her. She ended our relationship, and that devastated me. But I wasn't ready to face the consequences of my actions. I didn't know how to cope with the heartbreak, so I turned to the things that helped me numb the pain—mainly alcohol. I drank to excess. It started out as a few days a week and then I drank daily. That went on for years. She was my first love and high school sweetheart. Down the road, Zoe got mixed up in heavier drugs and struggled with diabetes. Tragically, my Zoe overdosed from heroine on September 20, 2022, and didn't make it. She will always hold a special place in my heart. I wish I could go back and know what I know now, lead as an example, love her correctly, and protect her. After the breakup, it all spiraled downhill for me.

By the time I had done ninth and tenth grades, each twice, I gave up on school and dropped out my junior year at 18. It all felt just too hard. I had completely given up on education and a lot of other things. I realize now that I had a mother wound of delayed gratification; I really struggled with this. Whatever Mom felt, is what I had to deal with. If Mom didn't feel like doing it, it didn't happen. I either got what I wanted right away from my mom, or I never got anything. I learned that behavior. Either I want it right now or I am not going to get it at all. It's how I acted because of what happened. I don't know when I will be okay or when I will feel good, because I didn't learn how by my parents. If I needed nurturing, no one was there to care for me. I didn't know where else I could get it, and I needed it right then. It's delayed gratification; and everything takes time, no matter what it is. The process is everything; and that's what creates results. I've created unnecessary pain and suffering just by being impatient with business, relationships, friends, and family. I have found that when insecurities and fear make my choices for me, it never produces the results I want and need. It is just not healthy.

At this point, I spent a lot of my time couch surfing; wherever I was partying that night, I ended up sleeping there. I just didn't want to stay at home. I had jobs here and there—like fast food, convenience stores, and a liquor store drive-through. One job I quit about an hour into my first shift. I asked for a break and my free meal, and just left. I was doing just enough to get by and to support my bad habits. I was completely unstable. I was a full-fledged addict by that time. My drugs of choice included alcohol, marijuana, and cocaine. I can't recall the first time I tried weed and coke, because it was just a big part of my life. I was a walking time bomb, full of anger, resentment, and pain from the constant poor choices that I made and that were being made around me.

My friends, Dave and Matt, and I looked for fights everywhere we went. We were hurting boys with our anger, and that is all we understood. I was arrested several times for fighting. One incident, I was in a bar and this young man went up to a friend of mine and hit him in the face. He pretty much sucker punched him. A security guard grabbed him right away and threw him out. My friend and I left shortly after to follow him. We turned the dark corner and there he was. We went up to him and my friend hit him first and knocked him down. Then I took off his boot and began hitting him with it. We later discovered this man escaped a facility and had a disability. I have such a huge heart for those with different abilities and when I discovered this news, it ate at my soul. I was stealing purses and anything valuable out of business offices. I wanted to buy drugs and alcohol. One day after taking a purse, I went by the river and dumped a lady's belongings after taking the money. Later I was arrested and in court I found out this woman had stage four cancer. I wish I could go back to these moments and undo it all. You never know what others are going through. Most of us carry all this pain and don't know how to be free and love. All I knew was rage at the time. I had felonies on assault and disorderly conduct. I was also arrested for possession of marijuana, stealing, and breaking and entering. Every weekend or so I was drinking, fighting, or getting into trouble. I was finally sent to Summit County Jail in Akron. Before going in, I was 5' 7" and 140 lbs. and being picked on and bullied. I went in looking like a little boy who had barely hit puberty. This wasn't play time and things all of sudden got real. If smaller guys in jail were being spoken to or taunted, they wouldn't hesitate to get up and start fighting. Little talk and immediate action. They had to—for protection. I had no father. Reality was here, and I was afraid. I was violated as a kid, abused by other men, and had no stable mother. Mom's husband, John, yelled and I would panic in fear. You're damn right I was going to learn how to fight back.

In lieu of going to prison, they sent me to a release program called the Oriana House in Akron. I was there for several months. Can you believe my mom, sister, and niece have all been locked up at this same place? Talk about a family tradition. I was experiencing a lot of fear and anxiety and it showed. When I was there, a 30-year-old Black brother and I shared a dorm room, and his bunk was next to mine. He was there dealing drugs. He saw the fear in me.

One day he asked me a question. "Hey man, why you do that with your head and neck like that?"

Embarrassed, I explained, "I have this thing when I have anxiety or get nervous, my head twitches."

"Aww man, you good. Don't be nervous, you gon' be alright."

He started to show me around, and really took me under his wing. He showed me the ropes, and one day in the bathroom while cutting his hair, he said,

"We gonna call you 16."

"What's 16?"

"16 switches.... like the hydraulics on my car... there are 16 switches."

He explained it to me, and we both laughed; he became like a big brother to me, and I felt safe. I felt okay to be me, and I knew he had my back.

One time, he took me with him to see his girl, and I watched her kid while they went in the other room to have sex. He taught me about women, schooled me on fighting, and took time to share his struggle with me. I felt like a G. I felt like one of these guys. I felt like I was a part of something, like a family or a tribe. It seems like no matter where I am, Black people have always seemed to have my back when I needed it. He didn't finish his time there and he ended up going to prison. I got out a couple of weeks later. By the time I was released, I was 6'2" and 200 lbs. I noticed that everyone who picked on me was smaller than me now... a lot smaller. I was confused and thought, "Wait, these were the same people bullying me and using racial slurs. Calling me a wigger." I realized then that I became a big bad ass; no one could pick on me anymore. Look at me wrong or mess with me, and I will bury you. Bring it, bitch! Although I was afraid inside, I learned that my external self could protect me now. For the first time, I was able to use *me* to protect *myself*. Now it was all about fending for myself. Protect, fight, survive. At that point in my life, I was just so angry at everyone and everything. It all flipped. I went from being a scared little pretty boy to a big angry young man.

In my early twenties, I lived a reckless life littered with bad decisions, drugs, and alcohol abuse—all driven by pain, hurt, and resentment. It was no coincidence that the women I dated lived similarly. People in bad situations are often drawn together, like two out-of-control trains headed for a collision. Sometimes they can find some moments of happiness together to block out the pain in the rest of their lives, but eventually they will crash and burn. All in all, little 'good' comes out of these relationships—and there are often major consequences.

Clearly, so much was building up inside of me and I needed a healthy outlet to deal with and express my anger and pain in a safe way. There was so much trauma and healing that had to be done. Trauma is a deeply distressing and disturbing experience. It's an emotional response to a horrible and terrifying event. I learned to deal with the trauma all by myself. Alone. Many of us have been hurt. You see, children don't get traumatized because they get hurt. Children get traumatized because they are alone with their hurt. I was born into the wilderness experiencing trauma after trauma. In the wild, you are left out in the open. I had no clue. I was just trying to survive and when I felt a threat, my internal alarms would set off and I was in fight mode. You see, when an event occurs that is perceived as a threat, stress, or frightening situation, the body's sympathetic nervous system is activated, adrenaline is released, and it triggers an acute stress response that prepares the body to fight, freeze, or flee. In other words, to stay and fight, be paralyzed, or run like hell.

I didn't know this then. I just knew that there was nowhere to go. Fight. Fight. Fight. Everything became a fight. It was unhealthy. All my reactions were an argument or a fight. There was nowhere to run. No safe place. This was my reality. The people who should have kept me safe were the very ones fighting with me. Here's the deal... my heart was severely wounded, and it was becoming hardened to the world around me. I was reaching out for anything, not even knowing what 'anything' was. It didn't matter anymore because if you got in my way, I got in your face. *Don't fuck with me. I will lay your ass out.* That was me – screaming at myself and hurting like hell inside. I lost control of my thoughts and actions. Depression and anger set in, and I didn't care a thing about anyone else's feelings. I was a walking tornado, get in my way and you will be destroyed.

My friends, Shorty, PJ, and Moe and I, along with a few other guys, decided to take a trip to San Diego. It sounded like a good idea, so I acted on my impulse. Shorty was a drug dealer. No one messed with him. The purpose of the trip was to go to Mexico so he could get a bunch of valiums and other pills. The first night we started drinking and hanging out in Tijuana. Moe and I met some girls there and hung out with them. At the end of the night, we were so drunk when we crossed the border back into San Diego. I remember holding a cab for us when a random guy tried to snatch it. Everyone had been drinking and were not in the right headspace. I told the guy that it was my cab, and he grabbed my shoulder and pushed me out of the way. I turned around and punched him directly in the face, knocking him out. Right away, the cops grabbed me, handcuffed me, and arrested me. There I was, barely legal, and in a jail in San Diego with a felony arrest on the very first night! The guy I hit was an off-duty MP (military police) officer in the army. I was facing years in prison over this one drunken decision. Here I was in the county jail again. As I entered the pod, I noticed the majority were Latinos and not Black and White, which was what I was used to. My court date was months out. I couldn't get hold of my friends, and they couldn't get hold of me. I had that moment when I believed my life was truly over. I'd waste away in a prison somewhere in California.

After about a week of trying to figure out my place in the California jail system where the politics were completely different, without notice, a guard came to get me out of my cell, telling me I was being released. I was shocked. As one of the officers handed me my release papers, he said that an elderly woman witnessed the event and on her own came up to the police station and made a report on what she had actually seen. I never met this lady and still have no idea who she is; for sure, my guardian angel. I got out of jail and went back home. So, there I was: my first vacation trip to California was spent in jail. Out of the friends that came with us, PJ is in prison; sadly, Moe and Jeff died of overdoses, and Shorty was found dead in a dumpster. They all died from very sad and tragic deaths. They were so young. I miss them every day.

Jason, Age 20 in Akron, Ohio

I was losing control to the point of wanting to end my own life. Being in the wilderness alone is not the best combination, even for a warrior. I knew I had to keep fighting to live.

I remember looking at myself in the mirror one night and a feeling of disgust washed over me. I hated the things I'd done, the way I was living and treating the people in my life. I took my own bare knuckles and punched myself directly in the face, dazing myself with all my rage. Sobbing, balled up on my living room floor, wasted, I felt completely irrelevant. I didn't want to keep on living. No one was home and I grabbed a shotgun from my mom's boyfriend's closet and put it in my mouth.

With tears streaming down my face, I tried to work up the nerve to pull the trigger, but I didn't do it. I couldn't. I had just enough will to keep living. Sometimes an ounce of willingness and faith of a mustard seed is all it takes. That's how willingness works. You think you have nothing left inside you, but you find the will. It's that voice in your head saying, *I want to do something, change something—badly*. Sometimes even a small bit of that wants to make a huge difference. We all come to a crossroad at some point in our lives when we need to make a choice. Whether the circumstances are good or bad, the way we choose to act (or not act) makes all the difference in the world.

Earlier, I mentioned my best friend from high school, David Hite. We sort of lost touch after we both dropped out. We got busy with life and never really connected again. At the time, we were both on a journey toward destruction. Somehow and somewhere along the way, David's path never got easier. Let me tell you what could happen when you let all that pain smolder.

One day a former classmate of mine reached out to me via Facebook and asked if I had heard the news. It turns out my good friend, David, continued on his path of destruction... and get a load of this... he actually found his father all those years later. The entire time his dad was in Cleveland while he was in Akron. As fate would have it, his father was a hard-core alcoholic, just like Dave. They ended up becoming buddies and connecting on that drinking level, but nothing deeper. The story goes that they were both done with their lives and made a suicide pact. The plan was for Dave to go to his father's house, drink heavily with his dad, and then they were both going to end the night by ending their lives. Well, Dave went first, in his father's living room. He took hold of the gun and shot himself. His father, most likely shocked, didn't follow through with it. No one really knows why. I ended up flying back to Ohio for David's open-casket funeral. He looked the same and at peace. I held his hand, crying, and leaning over his casket, asking why. Deep down inside I just wished we would've stayed in touch. I was so heartbroken for what his life could have been. If only he had been willing. That's right. If only he had the willingness to live another day. That's crazy, just a little bit of willingness can go so far.

Look, I don't know what type of situation you are in or how deep. You could be doing poorly in school, on the outs with your mom or dad about something stupid, not getting along with your siblings, being betrayed by your so-called friends, feeling worthless, and hating everyone (including yourself). Maybe you have already graduated and are looking for a job, or just got fired from a job you loved. Maybe you're trying to save money because you want to buy a car. Maybe you are finding that making new friends in a new city is not that easy. Perhaps you lost a child, or are going through a divorce, or betrayed by someone you truly loved. You've had it. You don't want to try anymore. And you are thinking that all of the struggles aren't worth it, and you are at the point of wanting to quit trying or even end your own life. STOP. PLEASE, just fight this emotional struggle a little longer. I feel you... I do.

I don't know what it is for you, but I do know that this is how far it can go if you let it. Just know that there is always another way, and it takes will to pull you through. When you agree to be willing, you agree to keep trying. It's a desire to pursue and fight for positive change in your life. This is the first principle of the My Warrior's Way. It's not time to quit. It can be as little as making that one call or putting that one drink down. Dave gave up, and by God, I wish he hadn't. Even though I, too, was sitting in my own living room; and I, too, had a gun in my mouth, I found the will to back off. I was willing to change my thoughts and behavior. I may not have completely understood why, but my willingness saved my life.

"The tragedy of life is what dies inside a man while he lives."

—Albert Schweitzer

CHAPTER 2
FIRE & DESIRE

A few months later, I faced another moment where I could choose to live or die. I got home at about three or four in the morning after a night of partying in Cleveland at a club called Trilogy. About three hours later, I heard chaos... and shortly after, John, my mom's new husband, busted my door open shouting, "*The house is burning down! Get out!*"

The entire house was catching on fire. Inside the house with me were my mom, John, my sister, my six-month-old niece, and our dog, Spike—a pit bull mix. We had to get out before it burned to the ground.

The area around me became hotter and hotter and the smoke continued to get thicker and blacker. There was only about 2-3 inches of light above the ground, and above me was black smoke and violent red flames. The second I took a breath, I choked. Suddenly, I knew I had to take some serious action, or else I would burn to death inside my house. I had a burst of God-sent energy. It was a three-story house, so I had to climb down the stairs in order to get out. I could barely see the pathway from the living room to the kitchen. I was terrified as I crawled on my hands and knees. Once I reached the kitchen, I was crawling over melting tiles. I had burns all over my hands and knees. A part of me was so panicked I didn't even want to continue crawling. I remember thinking, *my life is over.*

I was 21 years old. Something inside me wasn't ready to quit, so I scrambled as fast as I could through the flames and made it out the back door. I was the last one out. Everyone was already outside waiting for me. I was still slightly drunk when I made it out to where everyone else was. Sadly, Spike didn't make it, as the fire was raging by then and we knew we couldn't go back in. They found him under my niece's crib. I lost Spike and Kermie. I barely made it out myself. I was beginning to sound like a country song. My girlfriend left me, my dog died, and my house burned down. I was in the hospital with bandages around my burnt knees and hands, and on morphine. We never learned how the fire started.

Just a few months before, I was almost ready to end my own life, and now there I was, looking death square in the face. All I had to do was stop crawling and let the smoke and flames consume me, but I chose to take action. I wanted to save my life. My one action that night was a defining moment; it was going to cost me my life or cost me my death. There were no firefighters or family members coming in to help me out. It was just me and the fire. But there was a bigger flame inside of me. It sparked up, driving me out of the house. It was something I had never felt before. Was it scary for me to take that action to make my way out? Yes. What if my body caught on fire? What if I burned to death?

Knowing who I am today, the man I've become, I'm so thankful I never fired that shotgun into my mouth. I could have acted on my impulse to pull the trigger. I am so thankful I kept crawling out of that burning house. I could have curled up in a ball, like I had done so many other times when the stress got the best of me. The Red Cross put my family up in a nearby hotel. We all had separate rooms. I remember sitting up all night thinking about everything—what my life was turning into, where it was possibly headed, and where I wanted it to go. I just lost everything. My home and my clothes. I had nothing. I was still hurting from losing my first love, Zoe. I was depressed, confused, angry, and very sad; however, above all those emotions, I felt a burning desire for real change in my life.

But how could I change? I was a poor, uneducated 21-year-old kid from Ohio, and I knew nothing of the wider world around me. I lacked knowledge and money, and my life seemed hopeless. I was paralyzed by fear, but I saw clearly enough that I had only two options left: I could give up on life, or I could try something different. My willingness to pursue real change was there, front and center. I just had to figure out my next move. I needed to take action.

After the fire, I stayed with my friends, Shorty and PJ, for a few days in Kent, Ohio, trying to figure out what my next move was going to be. It was basically a drug house, a very bad situation, but one I was familiar with and understood. I was comfortable in this four-bedroom house. About fifteen of us lived there and it was a free-for-all. No rules. There were plenty of guns, various drugs, alcohol, and women. If you really wanted to party, that's where you wanted to be.

There I was drinking drugging again. I was messing around with several ladies and doing my best to be where the action was to numb all my pain and suffering. But then there was this one woman who told me she was pregnant and was pretty sure I was the father. We were deep into drinking and drugs and looking for a good time. Our relationship was casual. We were having fun, not making babies. I guess I could be the father, but at the time I thought, maybe, maybe not. No action needed. Sometimes weeks and months would pass before we would see each other again; but of course, I didn't think the child was mine. Just in case, I did go with her to a couple of doctor appointments at the beginning, but that was really the extent of my involvement. Being addicts, we weren't very thoughtful people.

I kept stepping into the same self-destructive lifestyle. Why was it so hard for me to understand that this wasn't serving my highest good? I didn't know anything else. And you know what? At the time it was comfortable because in my mind, it was safe to stay put; or so it seemed. It's scary stepping out into the unknown, and then having to venture off after being in the desert. At least it seemed that way to me. I was an untamed beast hating the world, numbing my pain with drinking, drugs, and women. I trusted no one. How could I? I had to find a way to feel good any way I could. I was on the road to nowhere. In fact, I was on the road to being locked up or dead. I was a dead man, walking. That's where I was headed.

One day at Shorty's house, there was a commotion going on outside in the front yard. I went to see what was happening, and as I stepped onto the porch, I saw a guy stab another guy. It was crazy. Everyone took off, and I booked it too. That's when it hit me. I finally understood what that burning desire was inside of me. It was a will to get myself out of that ugly war zone that was my world. I didn't know it at the time, but my Warrior spirit was showing itself for the first time. I had to muscle up, in a good way, and take action. Facing my fears dead in the face was my only option. That was all I had left inside me. Courage is what is needed to take on real change. Having a brave heart, even when it is wounded, can come alive at the most pivotal times of our lives.

I have since learned that all the things I have been through in my life were giving me a greater purpose. Before I learned that, I got caught up agreeing with the lies. Yes, those unfortunate and tragic things happened to me; but I know deep down in my Warrior spirit that they happened *for* me. We all need to go through life's challenges to find the Warrior inside that will lead us to our true purpose, because we all have one. Are you willing to wake up the true Warrior living inside of you? It means taking action.

I had a hard time trusting others. I took on the narrative that everyone wanted to take something from me without asking. In my mind, everyone was in it for themselves. If you don't have trust, you don't have anything. It all starts with trust. It always will. Whether it is with yourself, another relationship, or with a higher being. We aren't going to have someone operate on us if we don't feel good about it. Trust is everything. I replayed this tape in my mind and retold it over and over to myself that I couldn't trust anyone. I was alone, and I felt okay with that. If I don't trust anybody, then I can't get hurt anymore. I couldn't trust the woman who gave birth to me. It took a lot of hard work to get past that, and to this day I am conscious to not project this mistrust on to all women.

For real change to happen in my life, I would need to take drastic action. Willingness is the first step but without action, forget about it. It requires all of you. This is the second principle to the My Warrior's Way. Taking definite action has the possibility to enable physical, emotional,

"The path to success is to take the massive, determined action."

—Tony Robbins

and spiritual change.

I had to put the state of Ohio in my rearview mirror and enter into the unknown. I had no idea where I should go. I knew that the ideas simmering around in my crowded little head would be very uncomfortable, scary, even painful to act on. It would surely be easier just to stay somewhere in Ohio and hope things and people around me would change. But that wasn't going to happen. My hometown wasn't going to change, and the people around me had no desire to be different. It wasn't a safe place for me, so I had to flee. I knew it was time. *No mas.* Just like the boxing great, Roberto Duran, when he fought Sugar Ray Leonard, there was a moment when he knew it was over. Humbly aware, he knew the fight was bigger than himself. He put his gloves up and said, "*No mas. No mas.*" The ref wasn't saving him, but he made the choice to save himself. He knew he wasn't going to win the fight on that night. My fight, too, was over. I knew that after many rounds, I had to be done. *No mas.* There is nothing to be ashamed of when you stop fighting a battle that doesn't serve your long-term best interest – like a toxic relationship or using drugs on a regular basis. Sometimes changing your decisions can be the most heroic thing you will ever do for yourself and for others. It could be your greatest win. I really didn't know much of what went on outside of my little hometown, but the fire within me was lit. I knew that unless I took some serious action, and took it fast, my life would spiral out of control and into a downhill crash. What should I do? Where the hell could I go?

Do I really have what it takes, and can I do this all by myself? Another little secret, you don't have to know. In fact, you aren't supposed to know. Taking action into the unknown is ultimate courage. Birthing the ultimate warrior. Now, I'm not talking about WWF (World

Wrestling Federation) Ultimate Warrior back in the late 80's, although he was badass and the spirit of him shall live on forever. I'm referring to the ultimate you. And there will be times where we must face our deepest fears alone.

So here I am desperate and willing. I almost ended my own life twice and I'm only in my early twenties. It's time to make my desires happen by taking definite action.

COURAGE IS WHAT IS NEEDED TO TAKE ON REAL CHANGE

"Now you are out there. God knows where.
You are one of the walking wounded."

-Jan Krist, Walking Wounded

CHAPTER 3
THE WALKING WOUNDED

I knew I needed to get out, and fast! I needed to clean myself up and find a positive focus in life, but it was so challenging to just get up and go. I hadn't known anything else. The thing keeping me from taking the necessary steps was *FEAR: **F**alse **E**vidence **A**ppearing **R**eal.* I was conditioned and convinced to believe that I was an unlovable idiot, white trash, wigger, wannabe, unworthy loser, and nothing good was ever going to happen to me. I felt stuck, so why even try? I didn't have any real friends. What would I do with my life? How will I function were to even try? I was afraid of the unknown.

I kept fighting the battle in my head. You know what I mean? Giving myself the pros and cons of just about any new action I was taking on.

But I always wavered back and forth. From the reasons why, to the reasons why not. I was stuck in that quagmire of doubt and fear. The scriptures say perfect love drives out fear. Fear would keep me here, but love would drive me out. I believe that many times we make choices from two places: the fear in our heads and the love in our hearts. Bolting from Ohio in the middle of the night for places unfamiliar seemed ultra-risky on the surface, but I knew in my heart that staying there in that dead-end city was far riskier. As my vague plan to escape Ohio took shape, I remembered my visit to San Diego, California. And although I didn't see much and spent most of my time in jail, it was a place that stayed with me. My mom mentioned in passing a few times: California. When I watched all those beautiful people on the movie screen and on our small color television, they looked so cool, so suntanned, and so happy. They all seemed to be running around on a beach somewhere in Southern California. I always wanted to be awesome like them, to feel appreciated and loved, and to be happy. But the main reason I chose Los Angeles over other places like Florida or New York was because my mom thought that maybe my dad was there. She knew people who had moved to California, including one who might have been my father. So that's where I decided to go. I still felt a ton of fear once I made the decision to leave. I was excited and scared, but I knew I needed to make this move. And with everything else I had gone through in all my years of living on this Earth, things couldn't possibly get any worse... right?

In 1998, I was a 23-year-old man with no money in my pockets, big dreams in my head, and an imagination to think of all the possibilities. I had a cheap car, but it sure wasn't going to make it to California, so I sold my black Ford Laser for $2,000. This was all I had to start a new life. I felt a lot of fear when I sold that car. It freaked me out to take that first step. But after I made that move, the momentum of the situation took over. I couldn't afford a plane ticket, so I bought a ticket to take the cross-country journey on a greyhound bus, which took three days. There were things that could have gone wrong but didn't. I was ready and willing to make a change in my life, somehow. I took the cross-country journey to the City of Angels and boy was I in need of some angels. Shorty had a friend out in San Diego, and I thought I could stay with him for the time being but had no idea how far Hollywood was from there. The entire time I thought I was heading to Los Angeles. I left most of what I had been through behind in my small, depressing hometown. But I was still afraid. I've since learned that fear isn't what changes you. Pain is what makes you change. And I was in enough pain in my life that the fear of staying and experiencing more of that pain was far worse than the fear of leaving.

While sitting in my seat on that bumpy Greyhound bus, my mind was filled with all the dreams, ambitions, and visions of what I could do and who I could become. Staring out the window, my imagination was running wild with all of life's possibilities. But along with the whimsical dreams racing through my mind, I also had a harsh voice in my head, scolding me for dreaming so big. Who was I trying to fool? I was just some poor White-trash kid from Ohio. I didn't belong in L.A. I hadn't earned this. What great things had I done to warrant a great future? Nothing. That was my short and simple answer. In my heart, I considered myself a loser. I didn't deserve this at all. I felt shame and pain built permanent homes in my heart. They made sure I always remembered who I was and where I came from. This is the crap that crowded my mind on that long bus ride going cross-country. Extreme excitement about all the possibilities would take over, then I'd slingshot back into negativity. A pendulum out of control. I'd tell myself how I wasn't worth this experience and that I was simply running away. I'd convince myself that the journey to L.A. wasn't going to solve anything and that I was stupid for even trying such a silly stunt. What was I even doing?

What if? Just what if I was able to locate my father there? And what if my dad was a real celebrity like a lot of people who go to Hollywood? What if he's Brad Pitt? Or a loved famous actor? In my case, it would be more like Jim Carrey (good looking, but such a dork! Lol). Maybe one time he stopped in Ohio and hooked up with my mom. I know it sounds crazy, but *what if?* My mind was dreaming. Or what if I get there and someone sees how awesome I am and wants to star me in a movie? But then I would snap back into convincing myself that I was worthless. What if I end up poor and homeless, and no one is going to like me? My mind was like a tennis match, and I was swatting that racket back and forth, battling every negative thought or belief that got in my way. I struggled to stop the fight between my head and my heart.

I arrived in San Diego and couldn't believe how beautiful it was. Gorgeous sandy beaches, glamorous people, and expensive cars were everywhere. I stayed with Shorty's friend and immediately started to party with him, but soon realized it wasn't working out. We didn't get along. He was a hippie, and I was a thug. I have nothing against hippies; we just didn't see eye to eye. I got a motel in La Jolla, which is an expensive town nearby, but had no clue what was what. All I knew was that I needed somewhere to stay. I paid for a room for a month that took most of my money. At least I had a place to rest my head and sleep. At that point, I was overweight, and still insecure. I started drinking and using drugs even more than before I left Ohio. I drank most of my money away in the few weeks I was there. I had to find a way to eat and live. I didn't have a car, so I walked everywhere I needed to go... which was really nowhere because I didn't know enough yet to get around. Then one day

I noticed a group of men standing in the parking lot of Home Depot, away from the entrance. I asked them what they were doing. "We wait outside for the construction trucks to come out to hire us for work. They pay us in cash, so we wait here in the parking lot." I got up early the next morning and went to stand outside with the other men to see if I could get some work and a little money for the day. Looking back now, I'm sure I was quite the sight among those fifty or so Latino men waiting for work. I was just a young boy out there. It was one of those times where it was a disadvantage. The people seeking workers wanted men, not boys. They must have wondered, *what the hell is this young White kid doing here?* Many of the other workers left Mexico to move to the unknown to create opportunity and build a better life. That is exactly what I was trying to do by leaving Ohio. I respected them.

One day, one other guy and I were picked up to help an old man break up the concrete in his driveway and then toss it in a dumpster. I was paid 75 bucks for seven hours of hard labor, and I was glad. I went to the Home Depot parking lot every morning for the next week, but like many of us out there, I didn't get chosen for work every day. Some days I'd stand around for hours and make nothing. It was so damn frustrating, but at least I was taking some action. I kept moving and putting myself out there.

What happened? Well, I really wanted to find steady employment, and I channeled that desire into energy and actions. I left my name all over town with any business I thought would possibly hire me. I forced myself out of bed each morning to go stand in line with the day laborers waiting in the hot sun, sometimes for hours, for someone to pick me so I could make 50 or 80 bucks that day. The thought of standing in a Home Depot parking lot in the hot sun all day wasn't easy to accept, either. Anyone could look at me and see that I was struggling, but I was determined to get work. It wasn't a great feeling, but I knew I had to do something. I had to take action. I finally saved enough money to get another bus ticket and this time I was on my way straight to Hollywood.... The land of possibilities.

Sunny Los Angeles, here I come! I was so excited until I took a few steps off the bus and looked around. Homeless people were everywhere. My eyes searched for opportunities, but all I saw were prostitutes, drug addicts, and destitute beggars; virtually everything I was trying to escape from my hometown. I felt a sense of irony as I walked down Hollywood Boulevard, stepping over the legendary stars on the Walk of Fame, surrounded by such downtrodden people.

It didn't take me long to discover how expensive it was to live in California. We didn't have the internet or cell phones, like today, to quickly research anything, let alone the cost of living. I assumed it would be a little more money than Ohio, but it ended up being a lot more! I walked through the city for hours looking to find a FOR RENT sign hanging on a property I could afford, but everything was way out of my price range. Everything.

As the sun went down that first night in Los Angeles, I slept on the streets with my duffel bag. It was my first time having to make my bed on the cold pavement. Those were humble lessons right there. Am I going to make it? What was I doing? After another couple of days, I had enough money to make a call to one of my ex-girlfriends. Diane wired four hundred dollars to me through Western Union so I could get something to eat and find a place to stay. God bless her. It was enough for me to survive for a month.

I stayed at the St. Francis Motel on Hollywood Boulevard and Western. It was a dirty, rundown, drug addict–infested motel. There was no television, no refrigerator, and no air conditioning. It was disgusting, but it was the only place I could afford to sleep. I went to the nearby grocery store to buy water, a loaf of bread, peanut butter, and some pears. I ate those peanut butter sandwiches several times a day. I had no idea that this would be my daily diet for quite some time. Sadly, the kind older Black man that worked nights at the front desk was robbed and killed. They eventually closed that motel.

I didn't have a plan. I didn't have a job. I didn't have a friend. I didn't have a mentor. I looked and smelled terrible. I didn't know anyone in L.A. The only thing I knew for sure was that I didn't want to go back to Ohio—I couldn't go back. If I went back, my family and so-called friends would look at me like I was an absolute failure, and I would certainly feel like one. I knew I had to push through whatever obstacles or walls standing in front of me. Energy from deep down inside would be my savior.

Right away, I bought a skateboard because it was the cheapest thing on wheels, and I needed to get around. The first week in Los Angeles, as I was riding my skateboard down Hollywood Boulevard, I saw a movie set needing extras for a movie called *RAVE*. I stopped there and worked for the day. It was no pay, but they fed me. Two days later, there was a scene that needed a big, tall security guard, and so they asked me to put on a jacket and gave me lines. A week after being in LA, I am getting paid and with the screen actors guild. Being an actor was now something I was interested in. One of the actors owned a moving company and he hired me as a mover. So, I landed moving gigs here and there when he needed me. However, I knew I needed a steadier job. I applied at stores all over L.A. but got nothing. Time and money were running out, so I had to figure things out quickly. I put applications all over the city. Finally, my persistence paid off.

One morning, I received a call from the assistant manager at the local *Skechers* shoe store on Melrose Avenue. They wanted to interview me, and could you believe on my way there to the interview, a bicycle cop handed me a ticket for jaywalking? What the hell? I didn't even know what jaywalking was and now I had to pay for a ticket with no money. Thankfully, I must have charmed the pants off the *Skechers* manager because he hired me on the spot. I got the job and started a few days later.

Getting that job at *Skechers* wasn't easy. I lost track of job applications after about twenty-five. My interview clothes weren't great. I really couldn't afford a haircut. My lack of experience was an obstacle. And there were other challenges that had nothing to do with me, like people not hiring. All that rejection and lack of response was hard on my psyche. But because I'd put in the work, I was rewarded with the job at *Skechers*. This was a huge turning point for me. I felt like I had hit the big time because I didn't have to eat those damn peanut butter sandwiches and pears all day anymore. Even with a steady income, I still had to ration my money carefully. I had to make choices between getting two 40 oz. bottles of beer at night to unwind and having enough money for food later in the week. I wasn't used to having money in my pocket. As soon as I had enough money set aside for rent and food, the rest burned a hole in my pocket. I didn't save a dime. If I had money left over and saw a pair of sneakers I wanted, they were mine. I had zero thoughts about saving for a rainy day because, in my mind, every day was a rainy day.

So, eventually I began working at being responsible at the most basic level, like paying my bills and getting to work. That's it. But that was huge for me at the time. I never learned how to be responsible for a day in my life, until then. I know my mom meant well, and she did her best while battling her addictions, but she was unable to take responsibility for her life or (sadly) ours. I now had an obligation to something, and I was learning to have control over my role in my job. I was setting my alarm, waking up, and staying disciplined and consistent in getting there. Would it have helped to have had this training when I was younger? Absolutely.

Life can seem like a never-ending battle. It's a battle you can't win without taking personal responsibility for your daily and weekly decisions. This is the third principle I found in the My Warrior's Way. A warrior cares and has obligation over something or someone. I had to pull this mindset in when it came to my thoughts. I had to take responsibility over the constant battle of duty over my thoughts and actions. Most of my life, I blamed everyone else for everything; it didn't benefit me in any way. I could only control myself and my thoughts, which controls behavior. Blaming others for our problems never gets us anywhere. That attitude is understandable in a child, but as an adult it will only hold you back. It took me many years of counseling to learn this. I believe everyone could benefit from seeing a therapist, especially to help heal childhood wounds. Even though this was the beginning to understanding basic responsibility, I still had so much to learn.

I continued to struggle a lot during this time. I spread myself thin—financially, physically, and emotionally. And every single day I thought about how badly I wanted to go back home. I really missed my mom and my baby sister. It would have been the easiest thing to do. Even though I knew going back to Ohio would have meant failure, the thought still crept in. I told myself I could not go back. I'd been stuck in a black hole, and I had to get out for my own survival. I didn't have much confidence.

I was still trying to figure out who I was. But one thing was constant. I was ready for a big change, and I was determined to make it happen. No backing out now.

One change that came easy for me, mostly because of my environment, was my weight. When I lived in Ohio, I was overweight. All I did was drink and eat junk food. Once I moved to L.A. that all changed, and not necessarily because I wanted it to. I dropped weight quickly, largely due to my financial situation. I couldn't afford to drink as much or eat as much. Skateboarding and acting also motivated me. But there was also the fact that L.A. is flooded with very fit and healthy people. Almost everywhere I turned, there were beautiful people. So, I made the decision to start going to a gym. The fees were only $11 a month, and since I had stopped partying, I could afford it. I enjoyed it. It started to take the place of my addictions. I started working out a lot and playing basketball. I began to see physical changes in my body, and honestly, I started to feel better about myself. The job at *Skechers* lasted for only a few months. I walked into work one day and saw the police handcuffing my manager. Get a load of this. He had been stealing money from the store! Sometimes it's the boss who is the crooked one.

People in L.A. told me I had a great personality and should be a waiter. Waiters with a personality could make a lot of money. I took their advice and applied to local restaurants. Just after my manager was arrested, Tony Roma's restaurant called. I jumped at the chance; I was eager to see all those big tips each night. The job at Tony Roma's enabled me to save enough money to move from the run-down motel to a glorious three hundred square foot studio apartment. I was in heaven in that studio. I had a fridge, a sink, and a hot plate. I could make myself a hot meal. And, hey, the place was so small I could make that meal without getting out of my bed! I had a place to stay and a job. For the first time in my life, I was learning how to hold myself accountable and take responsibility for my living conditions, my finances, and my health. I had a decent job. I opened a bank account and saved a little money each week. I went to the gym. I finally saved enough to buy a car. There was good momentum in my life. Finally, at 25 years old.

Then I got a lead from my mom of possibly who my father might be. I researched his name for several months and searched in just about every city in California. I checked even the most remote cities, looked in phone books, and asked random people. I finally found his name in Santa Barbara. I got him on the phone and asked him the question.

"My name is Jason Hill, do you know Denise Hill from Columbus, Ohio?"

He responded quickly. "Yes, I know who she is."

My stomach dropped. I asked more questions like how tall he was and when he said he was 5'9" and had brown hair, I doubted that he was my father, although since mom has some height, I thought maybe it was possible. He agreed to a DNA test if I paid half, so I did. I was hopeful and nervous, wishing for it to be true. Unfortunately, the DNA test proved that he was not my father. All I wanted was a mentor or guide. Someone to help me get through my childhood and teach me how to have self-control and help me have a positive outlook. I had finally reached a turning point in my life, and I was learning how to make it on my own. I wanted and needed my father to be there for me. To this day, I haven't found my dad. I've spent my entire life wondering what could have truly become of me had he been around. Not knowing where you come from can mess with your identity and it sure did mess with mine. Who was I? Who was I as a man? What does that even look like?

At this point, because I lacked self-control and was making decent money, my drinking started to get out of hand again. Truth was, even though some things got better, I was hurt and insecure. Getting drunk was a good distraction from my pitiful life. At the time, the drinks seemed to be the poison that made me hella funny. In my mind it was just what the doctor ordered. I could get a crowd going. It felt good when friends of mine would tell me how funny I was. One guy said I should try doing stand-up comedy, which seemed like a good idea at the time, so I decided I would give it a shot. I knew I loved to see people laugh and be happy. So, why not?

My stage name was Jason Hill-*Yeah!* My first joke was introducing myself with that name and I always got a good laugh because of the way I presented it. "Thank you, guys! My name is Jason Hill-*Yeeaaaeaaaah!*" I know. I know. But back then it was funnier than you think, and it worked as my opener. Most of the jokes I wrote were dark, degrading, and derogatory, so I will not repeat them here... but, still... they sure did get me the laughs I was looking for!

Jason in Akron, Ohio, 1999

I started doing my comedy routine around different parts of Los Angeles. I was doing rather well, but there was a catch. Basically, I had to be highly buzzed or happily drunk before I would get up on that stage. That's right. The only way I could get in front of all those people and do my act to make them laugh was when I had the liquid courage running through my veins. One time I entered a comedy competition at the *Hollywood Casino*. The contest included Black guys and one White guy, and the host was Guy Tori. I was uncontrollably nervous up there on that stage. There were hundreds of people looking straight at me, and of course, I was loaded. Like all the other stage performances, I was having the time of my happy high life. I remember after the show a woman came up to me and said, "Baby, I just want you to know that you are very funny! But, boy! I bet you would be a hell of a lot funnier if you didn't drink so much of that liquor." The next morning, her words kept bouncing off the walls in my head. When I stopped to dissect what she was trying to say, I thought highly of her courage to approach me. And it worked. I should not have been drinking like that. That stranger was right. I was drinking for all the wrong reasons. I was only comfortable when I was loaded. I knew the right answer, but I was not willing to take the step.

Another location where I would occasionally perform was off 48th and Normandie at *M & M Soul Food*. A lot of the clubs I did were Black comedy clubs because I was comfortable there and it felt like home. They actually laughed with me, and I felt the love. Another spot was *Aunt Kizzy's Back Porch Soul Food* in South L.A. I would perform there frequently. A famous comedian, Rinaldo Ray, was the host, and after my set, he approached me to say, "Man... you a funny White boy, you know that? You have a lot of potential. Keep working on your stuff. I might want to manage you, but you got to chill on the drinking." So, there I was, a functioning, funny alcoholic who couldn't overcome stage fright and my own insecurities enough to see a path that could have landed me in the career of a lifetime, perhaps. Clearly, my problems sabotaged my intentions to get it right. Again, I was not willing to take that step. I sometimes think about getting back into comedy again. The world could use more laughter; that's for sure.

Shortly after that, I had the opportunity to make more money than I did at *Tony Roma's* at a new restaurant opening up called *The Saddle Ranch on Sunset*. They hired me as a mechanical bull operator and there were nights when I would leave work with $500 in tips in my pocket.

Sometimes less and sometimes more. My job was to party and make others party more. I was in the best shape of my life with 5.5% body fat, impressive abs, and big muscles. I was lean and mean. I was making more money, getting more women, and I had all the drinks I wanted. It gave me everything I desired and at the same time, filled my veins with a false identity and worth. Money, ladies, liquor, and a distorted sense of confidence. It clearly fed my ego.

I was there for about a year until one night there was a huge party at *The Saddle Ranch*, and a big fight broke out between a large group of people and a few of the waiters. I jumped in to help. A lot of us were let go the next day. On the outside, things were looking great, but I was still using drugs, feeling insecure, and was always angry. It just goes to show you, appearance isn't everything. You could chase perfection on the outside and care so much about what others think, but true joy comes from within. It is a choice and a deep trust that you can't get from the outside world. Insecurities can play out in all sorts of ways and mine played out at every turn I made. I had knee-jerk reactions to just about everything I did. How do I manage or eliminate all this? The money, women, sex, alcohol, and drugs? How do I do life and know what is good for me? I was still immature and needed a lot of guidance, but more importantly, deep down inside I still felt lost. There must be more to this. But what? This is when I started to think about becoming totally responsible for my thoughts, actions, and decisions.

"It's not the lack of resources that causes failure, it's the lack of resourcefulness that causes failure."

- Tony Robbins

CHAPTER 4

HEALING THE WOUNDS

I had been going to a few auditions here and there and wanted to secure an agent. This meant I needed some headshots. One day the photographer who did my headshots, Barbara, invited me to her church. She had a sparkle in her eyes that caught my attention. The only thing I knew about God growing up was that his last name was 'dammit'. As wonderful of a person Barbara was, I secretly hoped that maybe she would hook me up with some free pictures or a discount if I attended. She invited me to a Men's Day, and I decided to go. When I walked in, the first thing I noticed was that everyone was smiling and seemed to be happy. That felt weird to me and very uncomfortable. I honestly thought those people were faking it. I was tired of being let down by everyone and by life in general. I was allowing my past to color my present and my future.

It was a natural response for anyone who experienced what I had. Just as I was having these thoughts, a Filipino man named Leo walked up to me and introduced himself. He befriended me on the spot. I had no way of knowing then that Leo would alter the course of my life.

In that first conversation, Leo made me feel so much positivity and hope. He had a genuine interest in becoming my friend. That struck me as really foreign. I hadn't met a lot of people who just gave out compliments from the goodness of their hearts, and I worried about what Leo might be trying to trick me into doing by being nice to me. The sermon was about sins, and it scared me enough to question my choices. They asked me to come back, and I felt a desire to return. Leo asked me to lunch here and there, and because I couldn't refuse a free meal at that point in my life, I always said yes. I usually pretended I wasn't hungry, but the truth was, I couldn't afford to eat out very often. I think Leo knew that, and I remember one time in particular when he offered to share his guacamole with me. I think I devoured it within minutes.

One of the first things Leo did was take the time to learn about my background and my circumstances. We spent a lot of time talking about my problems and my beliefs about life. Leo is not a counselor nor an expert at giving advice. He is an introverted computer techie. He would ask me a bunch of questions, but all of it was genuine in getting to know me. His secret? He is an amazing listener. Over time, Leo would transform my way of thinking. He would help me learn to think and act like a stable and balanced young man. He could just as easily have given me a pat on the back and kept on moving, but I think he could sense I needed a lot more than that, and he took the actions no one else did.

For the first time in my life, someone really believed in me. As much as I wanted to guard my heart, I was inspired by his confidence in me and his actions that made the difference in my life. It's okay and good that you acknowledge that you have wounds and you have been hurt. You can work from the truth. Don't lie to yourself because if you do the wounds will not heal; they will just sit there and smolder.

Leo was a best man in Jasons wedding.

You have heard others say, *Just let it go.* No. I say *First, be with it.* Deal with it, feel those hurtful feelings and talk about it with someone who you trust. Heal from it. And then when you know you're ready, let it go. When I was hungry, Leo fed me. When I needed someone to talk to, he listened. When I needed a shoulder to cry on, he hugged me. And he didn't judge. Even when I told him about stuff I did in my past that I was truly ashamed of, he accepted me. He knew I was no longer hurting myself and other people around me like I had before, and he believed I was continuing to become a better person. Leo was my first mentor; I was 25 and he was 36. He opened the door to many resources for me. He showed his love by telling me that I was good enough. He spent time with me, listening without judgment. He helped me buy food if I was short on cash. I didn't know how to work hard and keep a job, or how to be a genuine friend to others. I was not even sure I knew how to be an honest and caring human being. I began to realize how truly broken and discouraged I was, emotionally and spiritually. I felt worthless. I thought I would always be a complete loser in every aspect of my life. I felt ugly from the inside out. Leo saw how hard I was trying. He knew that I needed help, and how easily I got discouraged. He understood that I was ready to quit once again.

We all need someone to believe in us when we're at our lowest, and we also need somebody to selflessly help us when we can't help ourselves. At that time, I needed help financially, emotionally, and physically. I needed a father-figure to love and care for me as if I were a boy again. Leo was there for me for all those things, like the good dad I never had.

With his guidance, I studied the teachings of the Bible and began to want to make changes in an effort to be more like him and those who followed the teachings of God. Through my conversations and studies with Leo about what I was learning, I found out that by the grace of God, I can heal and become a stable and balanced man. Fortunately, I have become that man through many years of therapy and counseling. Today, I enjoy having drinks with my friends and family from time to time, and the difference is now I am balanced, and all those 'highs' I was seeking are no longer necessary. I don't need to alter my head. I need to alter my actions. At the beginning, it was hard. I had to face the pain that I stuffed way down deep for many, many years. Anyone would run from it because real change involves real pain—but leads to a lot of real healing. If you can relate to what I am saying, you know the feeling

I'm talking about. For me, in the beginning, my anger problems kept creeping up. I learned how to survive among alcoholics, drug addicts, and thugs. Lie when you need to. When someone makes you mad, curse and yell at them. If that doesn't work, hit 'em. It wasn't unusual for me to get into an argument or even a fistfight, sometimes weekly. I was still mildly depressed and extremely insecure. Then life dealt me another crushing blow. A literal blow to the mouth.

I was playing basketball at a local park. Playing sports was a great outlet for me. It helped relieve the stress and anger balled up inside. But I got into it with another player who made me angry. Typical for me back then, right? To me, anything that didn't go well in life or in a game was always the other guy's fault. I never took responsibility for my own actions. Our game got aggressive. As I was trying to get the basketball out of the hands of this player from behind, he swung his elbow and hit me in my mouth—hard—knocking out several of my front teeth and shattering my gum bones. I was stunned. I ran to the bathroom mirror. I looked like a hockey player after the gloves came off. Back then, it was horrifying, but time changes things. When I look at those old photos now, all I see is a guy that looks like a young hillbilly, and it makes me laugh.

Now here I was, walking my big ass back home – bloody, furious, and with a couple of teeth knocked out of me. I made it home, but my apartment key was nowhere to be found. My roommate wasn't home or answering his phone. After putting my fist into the solid metal door, I was stuck sitting outside in the cold with my mouth busted up. I was locked out of my own damn apartment, and now with a swollen hurting fist. I was furious! I had been recently learning how to respond in my anger, and I then remembered Leo said I can always call him to talk through things. That is a healthier way to respond to my anger, and I needed someone to vent to, so I called Leo. He was kind, as always, and said, "I'll be right over to pick you up."

Leo took me to Patrick's house, who ran the Chemical Recovery group I was attending. We all dropped to our knees and prayed. Patrick told me that God's hand was on me, and that this was a battle I was not going to win. He was direct and straightforward. He provided something else I needed in my life: discipline and rules. Both men reminded me of the kind of drastic changes I was trying to make and at times they are not always easy, and sometimes life can just be hard. This was an obstacle, and I would run into more obstacles in life, but I know these two guys will always be there for me. When I fall, they will help me up. And for the moment, I was done fighting with myself and others; I was at the end of my rope. I finally humbled out and agreed to do everything I was told to do while in recovery.

Patrick and others who were running the Chemical Recovery group were incredibly strict and structured. It was just what I needed at the time. The start time for these weekly meetings were on Saturday mornings at 7:00 a.m. sharp. Not 7:01 a.m. One of the rules and non-negotiables was that you and your sponsor had to be on time. The point they drove home was that if you needed your fix, you would make damn sure you met your dealer on time or made it to the liquor store before they closed. So, as a member of the group if you or your sponsor were even one minute late, you couldn't attend. One morning, I was there on time, but my sponsor showed up late. They kindly let me know I had to leave. It was too late, and I couldn't be there for that meeting.

I went ballistic. "You've got to be joking, right? I get up at six in the morning on a Saturday and I show up on time in order to try to change my life and you are going to shut me out?"

They weren't budging. How could they do me dirty like that when I was there on time? It wasn't my fault. He was the one who was late; not me. Of course, now I understand what they were doing, but sure as hell not then. Well... guess what? I stood up full of rage, eyes wide open, and flipped them off with both hands in the air and said, "You know what? Fuck you guys."

On my way out the door, I flipped each one of them off, in their face saying, "Fuck you, fuck you, and fuck you." They all looked up at me, shocked, and none of them said a word. I blazed through the front door, started up my car, and my tires squealed as I accelerated fast to get out of there. A cop saw the entire thing and pulled me over. I was driving without a license and didn't have car insurance. Because of that, my license got suspended for a year. I called Leo boiling and told him everything. Calmly, he said, "You can borrow my 10-speed."

That really pissed me off but that's the kind of guy Leo is. He seems to be able to take any situation and problem and solve it peacefully, instead of having an emotional meltdown like I had learned growing up. Not only did he offer to pray for me, but he pointed me in the right direction and always offered me a solution... every time. He listened and began to problem solve with me like a father would do. He understood the pain I was going through, and he was just a phone call away. Because of him, I know the power of prayer.

One thing they made us do in Chemical Recovery that was very beneficial for me, was to write a journal of every drug I ever used and how it affected me and others. Basically, I found myself sharing my deepest, darkest moments with a big group of men. It took a lot of humility, grace, and courage to do that.

Everyone's frustration with life plays out in different ways. My frustrations played out in anger. Through counseling and my treasured mentors, I learned that when I was frustrated or angry, it was an opportunity to choose how to respond. One technique I use now to thoughtfully deal with frustration is box breathing. Breath-work is a game changer. It has the ability to regulate your nervous system. I inhale for four seconds. Pause and hold my inhalation for four seconds. Exhale for four seconds and hold my breath at the bottom of my exhale for four seconds. It's amazing what a few minutes of this breathing technique will do for your body and mind. And if that doesn't work, I'll just silently remove myself from the situation, gather my thoughts and emotions, and come back. It's so much harder to walk away from the battle, and sometimes it takes tremendous strength to not fight back. Now that is a wise warrior. Five to ten minutes... can you spare yourself the time to de-escalate? You're damn right you can.

I am also much quicker to accept when I don't know or understand something. Rather than become frustrated or angry at being stuck, I'll simply call or text somebody. I don't know everything. That's for sure. Usually, I'll reach out to a mentor and ask for some guidance. Over time, I learned that nothing worth having comes easy. Every good accomplishment in life requires effort.

A few weeks later, Leo picked me up for lunch. By this time, we were going out for a bite to eat once a week, to a place of his choosing. I loved this because it was always a nice place, and he always picked up the check. One day, we pulled into an office building on La Cienega Boulevard in Beverly Hills. I didn't see a restaurant, so I asked him where we were going. Leo told me he needed to stop and see a friend. We went up to the seventh floor and walked into a dental office. Leo greeted someone, and they stepped inside an office to talk. When they emerged, the dentist asked me what happened to my front teeth. I told him, and we talked for a little while.

"We could probably fix up those teeth, get them looking normal," the man said. "Can I take a quick look at them?" I agreed, but I quickly told him that I couldn't afford any kind of dental work. He brushed me off, saying something about a discount. The staff escorted me to an exam chair, shot a few x-rays, took impressions, and did a consultation. The dentist came back with the proposal to restore my front teeth. The work was going to cost over $7,000, even with the discount. Did you hear that? SEVEN THOUSAND DOLLARS! I felt completely dejected. It would be years before I could afford to have my teeth fixed. I went back to the lobby with the proposal.

"I'm assuming you can't afford this," the dentist said.

Embarrassed, I told him he was right.

"Leo told me about you. That you're a really great guy, and you're trying hard to get your life together."

I felt unworthy, but also proud that Leo said that about me.

"How about this," he offered. "You keep trying to get your life together. You work hard on that, and Leo and I will figure out how to take care of this. How does that sound?"

"*Wait, what?*" I thought. *Did I just hear that right?*

We'll get you some brand-new replacement teeth and your smile will look even better than it did before," he said. Standing next to the dentist, Leo shot a glance at me.

"No, Leo, I can't let you do this," I said. Of course, I wanted my teeth fixed. I didn't want to look like a hillbilly. But I still had a really hard time accepting help and love from other people. Looking back now, I know it was a mixture of pride and the feeling that I wasn't worth nearly that much money.

"It's already done, already decided, Jason," Leo said. He knew me so well by that time. "Just let us help you."

I felt so many emotions, so cared about. I was overwhelmed with gratitude, and I felt so loved. *Who does this?* It wasn't the money, although it was a lot of money. It was the act. It was mind-blowing to me to think that somebody would do this for a person they've only known for a short time. I'll never forget the feeling in my heart that day. It was the first time in my young life that I ever felt honest and unconditional love from an adult male. Leo was my first mentor, and he opened the door to many resources for me. He showed his love for me by telling me that I was good enough. He spent time with me, listening without judgment. He helped me buy food if I was short on cash. He eventually bought me new front teeth. He showed me love, not just through his words, but more importantly, by his actions. People like Leo who have been strategically placed into my life are by far my most valuable resources. But their showing up was, and continues to be, only half the battle.

The other half was about me knowing what I needed, recognizing their value, and accepting their help. I had to let go of the feeling of being a worthless or an unworthy person and allow them into my life. Still, Leo had a very different outlook in mind for me. He wisely advised me that the events of my past didn't matter. All that mattered was what I did from that day forward. He assured me that I was worthy of having a good life and being loved. Leo gave me permission to try these beliefs on for size. It was hard at first. I didn't think he really understood me or all the horrible things I had done in my past. But he did. He saw me for who I had been, and who I was becoming.

That was when the healing process began. When you don't deal with stuff, you are walking around like a wounded warrior. You are vulnerable, like an easy target to be taken out. You are unequipped and unprepared. And every day you are fighting to save your life. Now, stop for a minute. What happens when you are wounded? I will tell you what happened to me. I felt the stinging pain every day. So, I eased it with my steady desire for drugs and women, just to distract me from myself. I ask you, is that a remedy?

Clearly, if you have been reading this far you can see I was wounded from the get-go. There are cracks in my heart so deep, that the battle to heal was and still is an extraordinary feat that is always so worth it. The healing process is a continuous lifelong journey. For some boys and young men who are reading this book, this awareness may not manifest in your mind because we grow up feeling like we must always fight our way out of something. Question: Who has time to deal with feelings? Answer: All of us. To heal from a wounded heart, you must first acknowledge it is wounded and not just angry; and next you must pay attention to how you handle your wounded anger, feelings, and emotions. Take notes on your daily behavior and thoughts. What's really bugging you? Write it down to get it out of your system.

I was able to learn from God, church, the scriptures, my Chemical Recovery group, other men, Leo, and real mentors. I identified and used the tools I needed to heal and be my best. This is being resourceful, the 4th principle to the My Warrior's Way. Find yours and become it. We all need mentors, coaches, and people who have gone before us to help provide guidance. Yes, you have your own intuition and wisdom, but there are times when life gets messy, and your perceptions may be cloudy. It's imperative that you build trusting relationships, practice vulnerability; and with humility, listen to what others have to say. We all have areas we can improve in, but that doesn't change our value. We don't need to spend our time and energy impressing others by being puppets. Listen to what they have to say and ask yourself, *Will this help me become my best?* If it matches up, follow it. Sometimes we are so much in a funk that we just need that little push and support. It sounds too simple, right? But for a kid who never truly felt safe or genuinely cared for before, it was profound. It's amazing what another person's belief in you can do. Without Leo loving and believing in me, I don't think much else would have been possible. He gave me a new vision. Now, he would never take credit for this. He's a well-grounded man. But seeing the way he lived his life and watching him interact with his wife and kids inspired me. Leo reminded me that I could put my faith and trust in God's plan for my life. I didn't have to shoulder everything alone. I could pray and put myself in God's hands. I believe a sense of spirituality is essential for anyone trying to make improvements and overcome trauma.

Everything happens for a reason, and I truly believe God brought Leo to me to inspire me and show me what unconditional love means. In her book, *The Gift of Imperfection*, Brené Brown expresses this perfectly:

Feelings of hopelessness, fear, blame, pain, discomfort, vulnerability, and disconnection sabotage resilience. The only experience that seems broad and fierce enough to combat a list like that is the belief that we're all in this together and that something greater than us has the capacity to bring love and compassion into our lives.

Spirituality is recognizing and celebrating that we are all inextricably connected to each other by a power greater than all of us, and that our connection to that power and to one another is grounded in love and compassion. Practicing spirituality brings a sense of perspective, meaning, and purpose to our lives.

One thing I know for sure is that I needed to forgive all those people who did me wrong and all the unjust things that happened to me. I learned that forgiving is not for the other person. It is for me. You can't truly embark on your warrior's way through your journey without forgiveness, you will never reach the full benefit. Let me explain. If I cannot forgive those who wronged me, then my heart is still wounded. If my wounded heart is the root of my strength, I will always be in a state of bitterness and resentment, and in the exact spot, which is hard to overcome. I have done this exercise, and recommend you try it, too, if you are working through forgiveness. Most people can't heal from things because they simply don't deal with those things. Make a list of wounds you feel others have caused you. Write them out. Then write a letter to them on how it all made you feel, how you responded to life because of it, and most importantly—be real. If things were not ok, let them know in your letter. Tell them what this part of your story has taught you and how it has served you. Thank them and if you can, forgive them. It is a hard thing to do, but tremendously important for the heart of a warrior. Or seek out a grief specialist to help. It's important not to rush the forgiving process either. Sometimes it takes many years to fully forgive, and that's ok. But the longer you wait, the less free you are. We don't necessarily forgive to free the other person; we really forgive to free ourselves. My mother was a major source of pain and suffering for most of my life, but through a lot of personal effort on my part and a lot of patience through my suffering, I have fully and completely forgiven her. I just took her to see Dave Chapelle and we had the time of our lives laughing the entire night, and although it took over 40 years of my life to experience my mom sober and happy again, I am a proud son. My beautiful mother didn't get sober until she was almost 70 years old, but let me tell you something... I got to understand a little bit more about

MOST PEOPLE CAN'T HEAL FROM THINGS BECAUSE THEY SIMPLY DON'T DEAL WITH THOSE THINGS

her and her story. I have a new level of compassion and empathy that didn't exist before. Do the work; it's a powerful choice to strengthen the heart and the mind of the Warrior you are becoming. The point is, don't put it off any longer. Deal with it and heal from it. You got this, Warrior.

Later, on March 28th, 2001, I was baptized, which also happened to be my baby sister Amanda's birthday. I was 26 years old. I became sober and stopped using recreational drugs and put an end to my bad drinking habits. Many challenges were ahead for me, but it felt like the positive changes I was looking for were beginning to materialize. I believe it was happening because I had finally shown I was willing to build on all that I was learning and put in the work. My childhood environment created one version of me. I was changing into someone new. Love is about action, not just feelings. What kind of action? The Bible says it best:

"Love is patient, love is kind. It does not envy, it does not boast, it is not proud. It does not dishonor others, it is not self-seeking, it is not easily angered, it keeps no record of wrongs. Love does not delight in evil but rejoices with the truth. It always protects, always trusts, always hopes, always perseveres."
—1 Corinthians 13:4

Sometimes we get wrapped up in our day-to-day struggles and forget about love, receiving, and giving. But love is the most basic resource every human being needs. Now I had love and other resources. People can be a great resource, especially when you have community. There is a lot of shared wisdom, support, and encouragement. Resources and resourcefulness are two different things. Nobody was holding a gun to my head when I walked into that church, curious and open to God's message of love. I took the first step in identifying resources, and then I used what was offered to me. I got past some of the shame and became open to accepting a little help and another person's unconditional love.

I was becoming a resourceful person as I battled to overcome addictions. I have worked hard to pay that forward ever since.

I also had to focus on believing if God was real or not. With the kind of life I have lived, it was (and sometimes is) hard for me to do that. Are you really here, God? One time, I saw someone praying the same thing and thought, "Yup, is this all a bunch of bull crap or what?" I did not have the evidence I needed to be convinced, so it was like a ping-pong battle in my head between big faith and no faith. My heart believes it to be true, but my head is trying to let go of the emotions attached to some of the stuff that happened to me. Through it all, one question runs back and forth across my mind. Could the Bible and God become my guidebook and my Father? Definitely. Now I want to be clear here, I still battle to "believe" in God, or more specifically… religion. Yeah, religion has hurt so many in history. I know there is a higher power out there. Whether it be God or the universe. I just know we are all from the same "Source." I certainly don't ever want to come off as a Bible basher or know it all because I don't. I do however believe and accept all humans as they are and whatever they believe. We are ALL connected.

I was beginning to transform my life into something good and discover a higher purpose. Now my consciousness was burning… my heart needed to know. Did I truly have a daughter out there? It wasn't long before I was overcome with a sense of guilt and shame. Was that little girl born in Ohio really mine?

"Nothing worth having comes without some kind of fight."

—Bruce Cockburn

CHAPTER 5
A WORTHY BATTLE

It started with me learning how to pray to my Maker. I would ask God to reveal the truth to me. I called the woman who claimed I was the father of her child. I finally decided that I had to know for certain. I went back to Ohio to get a DNA test, then headed back to California. It was a long three-day drive from Ohio to the west coast. My sister paged me while I was driving through Las Vegas to say the results came back. I pulled into *Harrah's Casino* to call her back from a pay phone. She picked up on the first ring and asked if I wanted her to open the envelope and read it. Of course, I said, "Open it! Open it!"

"The test is 99.95% positive."

"What does that mean? I don't get it."

"You are the guy. You are her father for sure."

I was overwhelmed with emotion; I could not speak. Dead silence. She was mine. Ana was my daughter. I have a kid. Holy of all Holies! I am a father.

But once I knew about my child, I was facing some of the same decisions my mom had to make. Do I take responsibility for the life that I created? How do I even do that? I don't know anything about raising children. It's not like I had the Brady Bunch model in my home. I have been reckless most of my life, and I was scared, but also so excited! It still pains me to not have been present at her birth. This news added to my desire to change and start taking responsibility for who I was and my new-found daughter. I'm in California and my new baby girl is in Ohio. At that moment, I wanted to meet her, and I had an immediate feeling in my gut that now I had a purpose and someone to care about and care for.

Suddenly, I felt a tremendous amount of inspiration to be something I never had for myself: a father. How am I supposed to do this? What does this look like? I had a lot of questions and no idea where to turn for advice. At night in my three-hundred-square-foot studio apartment in Hollywood, I would sometimes cry out of pity for myself and how my life was turning out. I did not want to do what was done to me. But one night, my cries were different. I didn't cry out for poor Jason. I found myself crying out to my Creator, a higher being: God, who gave me life. I begged for direction and help. I was tired and broken. What I asked for in my cries and prayers was the courage to face my challenges. I asked God for the kind of toughness I needed to change my life so I could love, care, and protect this little girl we created. Not tough on the street or on the basketball court; it was the toughness in my heart. I also asked

God for the relentless strength it would require to give my child the opportunity to know and have a good father. I was in my dark room with no lights on. My bedroom windows at the time were blacked out. At the final end of my prayer, I said,

"God or whoever made me into existence, if you are real show me."

You must believe me when I tell you this. Without warning, the entire room was vibrating with a bright orange light, and it was glowing. There was a warm feeling as the light filled the room. There was also a sound that seemed like it came from another dimension. It's hard to explain, except to say that I felt suspended in time. It was the closest thing to floating I have ever been. I closed my eyes and covered my face. I couldn't believe it. Believe me when I tell you, I wasn't on anything. I peeked out from under my covers, and I was freaking out. What the....? What is happening right now? I got spooked and looked again and sure enough, something was going on. I said, "Okay, God. I will do whatever you ask me to do." It lasted for a few minutes, and then it was over. I needed a sign to know that He was real and after that moment I knew. I took immediate action. This was the most real thing that ever happened to me. I leaned in to find out that God and the Universe had my back. It was going to be a tough road ahead, but I was ready. I promise you, when you go through your moment, you, too, will have a story to tell.

Learning that I had a daughter was petrifying on all levels, but it was the best damn thing that could have ever happened to me. Until she was born, my life had zero purpose. I was just alive, and honestly sort of an angry lost zombie. I will admit, the beginning was an extremely difficult and frustrating time in my life that would last for several years

There were countless flights back and forth from Cali to Ohio for visits and court battles. Year after year, I would keep going back and her mom wouldn't let me see her. There was so much drama. I realized the only way I would be able to maintain a relationship with my daughter is if I fought for full custody. My baby's mama didn't like that I was all in for this battle. I want to believe that my dad would have fought for me, if he knew I existed. This little girl was mine and there was no giving up. Although, I wasn't perfect, I was determined to get her out of that environment. This little girl was now changing my life and woke up the warrior in me. She was my beauty to rescue. At least once a week, I had gone from fighting someone in the streets to now redirecting that energy into fighting for my little girl.

First, I was granted visitation and phone calls, and Ana's mom didn't like that either. When I would call on my days she would say, "Ana, your fuckin' father is on the phone." That is my baby girl's first impression of her father. Her mom would constantly talk bad about me. When I would call, Ana would feel anxious. She knew I was her daddy, but she acted as if I was just a stranger who she has been taught to dislike. It was a challenge to win her love because she knew me as someone I was not. Her mom's view of me became her view. Ana looked at me with suspicion filled with tension, like—who are you? I have to go with *you*? She would look at her mom and say, "I don't want to go with him." Although Ana was my hero, I really wasn't hers. I was painted as a villain, but I was the furthest thing from that. Ana acted out when she was around me, and understandably so. She would hide when I showed up and it broke my heart. Not only was it a battle in the courts, but a battle for my little girl's heart. One day when she was 5 ½ years old, I was driving her back to her mother's house, and I asked her a surprising question. "Ana, why are you so mean to me?"

"My brain just tells me that I don't like you," she said.

Those words felt like an actual knife had just sliced my heart. The first few years of getting to know my daughter was challenging because as thrilled as I was to be with her, it was the opposite for her, and it was hard to witness. This beautiful innocent little girl was full of worry and anxiety. A child's development between the ages of 0-5 years old is huge and most of their belief system is cemented in. She heard her mom cursing and using abusive language filled with a tone of resentment, anger, and bitterness. I needed to gain her trust. Her mom was an addict and didn't like me at all. She spoke terribly about me in front of her. I went back to see Ana on one of the visits and she was gone and not in Ohio anymore. Her mom took her to Florida without telling anyone. She packed her car up and left with her boyfriend along with Ana. During this process, Ana's grandparents (mom side) and I had to put our heads together to figure out what we were going to do. Somehow, we were able to convince Ana's mom to let her stay with her grandparents for the summer. At the time, Ana was around 6 years old. Well, that was a huge opportunity for me to visit with my daughter. Really, it was the beginning of building a relationship with her under healthy circumstances. Her grandparents were in favor of me spending time with her, so that helped. Ana didn't ask for or deserve these challenges.

Visiting my beloved daughter Ana in Ohio

I was living with one of my best friends, Allan Avendano, at the time. He was so thoughtful and caring. He has to be one of the most amazing souls on the planet. For my birthday, he surprised me. He helped gather friends together to pitch in for a plane ticket to Ohio so I could see my daughter. He was one of the best things that happened to me and Ana. When I was gone for a couple of days, he put frames and artwork up with photos of Ana in them. When I returned home, my daughter's pictures that now covered my bedroom walls inspired me to keep fighting. *Don't quit, Jason. Thank you, Allan.* Talk about having a huge heart! He encouraged more friends to write letters to the court about my character so I could show the judge that she needed to be with me.

During this long, drawn-out battle, I started dating women inside the church. And this was a different type of dating than what I knew. One of the tenets of the church was that the purpose of dating was to encourage one another, and it didn't necessarily have to be romantic. If it turned into that, cool. Regardless, it had to be chaperoned with another couple or be a big group date. To be clear, it had to be done the church's way. If it wasn't, then you would get talked to.

On the 4th of July, the singles ministry in my church was hosting an event and friends were getting together to head to Castaic Lake to watch some fireworks. What a show! The fireworks lit up the sky. At the time, I was sporting that cool bleached-blond look. I also had a cast on my knee and was on crutches, thanks to some torn ligaments from a basketball game. So, there I was, hobbling around the park when I first saw Vanessa. She was sitting on a blanket, playing cards with one of her friends. I locked onto her big brown eyes and silky caramel skin. She was beautiful, a stunning Latina woman with the most inviting smile. She came to the event with her friends from church.

"Wow. Who is that?"

"Oh, I know her. That's Vanessa from West Covina," said my friend, Allan.

I made my way over and began talking to her with whatever game I could pull out of my head. I must have been a sight, and I'm not sure she was overly impressed with Jason Hill. But a year later, we started formally dating. Things really clicked and accelerated after that. I was growing, but deep down inside I was still that little hood kid from Ohio with no formal education. Vanessa, on the other hand, graduated from her high school with honors and was senior class president. When I met her, she had recently graduated from college. Talk about academic polar opposites! Her educational background was appealing to me because I had none. I wanted that kind of person around me. I wanted a stable and balanced woman in my life because I'd never experienced anything like that before. I wanted emotional peace and heightened thinking, and to truly experience normalcy; something that I have seen in other couples and families in our church.

The church we attended was all-encompassing in our lives. Their views and rules on pre-marital relationships were simple and straightforward: no dating outside of the church and no kissing or sex before marriage. If we decided not to adhere to church rules, we would be publicly rebuked, shunned, and most likely asked to stop seeing each other and possibly even asked to leave. That's how strict it was. I was still just a kid from the streets of Ohio, so when the voice in my head told me to listen to the church leaders, I did. This had become my default mechanism so I wouldn't make another dumb decision. In this particular church there was no room for mistakes, and little room to make your own decisions. We simply obeyed the rules and protocols, even when we didn't understand them, or they didn't make sense to us. I became a product of exactly what the leadership of the church wanted: a robot. I didn't want to mess up at all. I was especially terrified of the leadership staff. We were so obedient because obeying church leadership was equal to being a "Godly person."

Disappointing God and our church leadership was the last thing Vanessa and I wanted to do. Any measure of independent thought flew out the window. In this church, you made "God decisions" or you were disappointing your Creator, and that came with some heavy consequences. Of course, when you are neck-deep in a church or organization that doesn't allow for independent thinking, you are not really making your own choices. You're making choices that please others, and hopefully God. But those choices can have some damn heavy prices to pay. I made one of those choices, seemingly simple and small, that I thought was pleasing those around me and God.

I remember the day so clearly. Vanessa and I were standing in the street I lived on, Carlton Way, in Hollywood, California. She and I were talking to each other in front of her parked car.

"There is such a chemistry and connection between us, don't you feel it?" she asked.

The first honest thought that popped into my head was, "Not really, no." But what I actually said was, "Yes, I do." She was just such a beautiful woman, inside and out and I couldn't have chosen a more perfect woman to have around my daughter, so how could I say no? I spent my whole life making bad decisions. This was not the first time I listened to my head rather than my heart. At the time, I thought this was the best thing.

I should've been aware and mature enough to speak my true feelings, but that wasn't how I allowed myself to be programmed at the time. Because of the cult-like reverence I had for our church leadership, I didn't want to disappoint them and God. In that exact moment, I knew that I wasn't truly in love with Vanessa. Many years later, I would learn that she wasn't truly in love with me, either. I was so desperate to have something whole and meaningful. Deep down I wanted my own loving family. I guess at the time, I would've done anything for love, even if it wasn't the real deal. We were just two young adults searching for something meaningful, wanting what we believed others had, yet afraid to be ourselves and make our own decisions. Instead, we abided by our church rules.

From the moment we started dating, her family welcomed me as one of their own. Vanessa is Mexican and has a very big family, and at the time they all lived in Los Angeles. They would get together almost weekly just to spend time with one another. Growing up, I had never experienced anything like that. The Garcia side and her mom's side of the family both gave me something I always desired: a real and loving family environment. This was my first true experience of family love. Oh my God, I can't even tell you – everybody hugged and kissed and looked into each other's eyes. They laughed, barbecued, and came together for no particular reason, then did it all over again the next week.

They would rent those bouncy houses for the kids to have fun. It was happy and beautiful. They took me in as their own. I would always dream and wish I had grown up like them. It was so warm and comfortable. I never felt like I was this White guy trying to fit in. I felt like I belonged.

One day, my new Uncle Hugo told me, "We're gonna call you "Miklo," and everybody laughed. I had no idea what that meant, so later I found out that Miklo was a White man with blond hair and blue eyes who had an abusive White father and a Mexican mother. The character, "Miklo," is from the movie, "Blood In, Blood Out." In the movie, his friends also referred to him as "El Guero," which in Spanish means White guy. Miklo looked very Caucasian. Yes, he was White, but he was also half Mexican. He resented the White part of him because others didn't accept his outward appearance and skin color. Even though he was actually only part Latino, his soul was one hundred percent Mexican, and he was extremely proud. He had to fight to be himself and accepted by his environment only because he didn't have the same skin tone as them. As a White-looking man living in a Mexican world in inner city Los Angeles, Miklo remained authentic to himself, despite his challenges. His White father abused him, both physically and emotionally. It was his way of toughening up his son. On the street, he was misunderstood and never accepted as a "true Mexican," except by his few very close friends who embraced him as he was. This had a major effect on him throughout his life. So, I really related to that part of his character. Eventually, Miklo became the head of the largest Mexican gang in San Quentin prison.

This was the beginning of something beautiful and would shape and heal my wounded heart. What I have learned about myself is that basically, I'm a White guy who enjoys and desires being around everyone. All people. All colors. All ethnicities. All types. Through my memories of being "raised" by the people around me, my heart and soul have embraced the love and nurturing from those many different cultures that truly embraced me as I was. Black, Filipino, and Latino cultures have made special homes in my heart. They all made me feel accepted and very loved, which was cultivated from a very young age, and it continues to this day. Plus, they always feed me well. Have you ever eaten authentic Soul or Mexican food? Chile con carne? Wow. Ask your Black or Mexican friends to have you over for a home cooked meal, you'll understand what I mean. Yo, I know that might come off as impolite to self-invite but let me tell you, if they love you, they will have you. Their food is unreal.

This brings me to what I value most and why. For me, it's family. Not relatives; that's completely different. Vanessa met Ana a few times and fell in love with her. I wanted a family, and this was all starting to feel really good. One day, Ana was taking a bubble bath with her toys, and I asked her if I should marry Vanessa and she nodded her head with a big smile and said yes. That was all I needed to seal the deal. It was eight months from our first date to our wedding date. Ana was our flower girl and she looked like an angel. We were desperately waiting for everything to get finalized with the courts so Ana could make her way to us. Only two people from my blood family, my cousin and my aunt, attended my wedding. And that was only because my aunt happened to be in California that week to see her son, my cousin, in San Diego. Nope, my mom did not come, neither did my sister or my grandma. No one. This was my wedding. I was embarrassed because I basically felt like I had to have a sympathy plea bargain, asking my aunt to drive up three hours to light the candle for my side of the family. At the wedding reception, however, Vanessa's entire family was present: cousins, aunts, uncles, grandparents, and neighbors. There were probably two hundred people or more there.

Ana and Vanessa at the weddng

I have a few blood relatives, but we rarely speak to each other. I love them and care for them because we are on the same family tree. Although I have known them my entire life, I have never really been close to them. Even so, we have a good relationship and stay in touch. This was everything I wanted and longed for. A real family, spiritual guidance and support, and a beautiful, kind, and educated woman who never got drunk, used drugs, or did anything unbecoming. She loved Ana and treated her so wonderfully. So, I married her. Of course, on the outside it was the perfect story we both bought into. We lived in West Hollywood our first year, and we got along well and really didn't argue too much.

To be honest, I was living for the story. I was determined to build a life for my precious little daughter, but it wasn't my truth. Living in your truth is everything, whether it is with your family, job, organization, or your loved one. Are you people-pleasing? Are you afraid that if you say what's real for you, you may risk a loss? The truth can be painful to look at, but it can set you free. Most people can't handle the truth. The truth hurts because it calls on you to make tough decisions about you and you alone. Many decisions are based on pleasing your family, a friend, a boss, a pastor, and so many others – even though you're hiding a big lie underneath it all. Pastors have affairs, millionaires steal, and inauthenticity seems to be the norm nowadays. I would bet that you, too, have experienced brokenness at some time in your life. Don't hide. Don't compromise and don't settle for anything or anyone. Be real so you can heal and live an authentic life. This may require you to make some very tough decisions that may seem wrong or crazy to some, but for you – it's your truth and your happiness. Honestly, I would like you to pay attention to yourself, listen to yourself, and trust your gut. Live your life, and not the story that others have created for you.

Toward the end of our first year of marriage, Vanessa and I made the decision to help serve in our pre-teen ministry. We just fell in love with the kids so much. We ended up following those kids and graduated with them into the junior high ministry and then into their teens. That was really a great gift to grow with them and watch them take on life. We mentored and studied the Bible and became close to the kids and their families. I realized that this was just what I needed when I was growing up. For Vanessa and me, attending those summer youth camps was something we always looked forward to. We just loved being with the youth. Every teen and family were precious gifts to both of us.

I soon realized that the intention and idea of support was great from our church, but it was conditional. Being safe needed to be real, especially for the youth, and it wasn't. They needed reassurance that being there was worthwhile, and the church did very little to get them interested or hooked onto a feeling of brotherhood among their peers. It was all about behavior modification. Preach. Preach. Preach. At the time, I didn't know any better. No one should ever have to feel like they need to be somebody they are not or not welcomed because they are not fitting into a preconceived mold. We should love and accept everyone unconditionally, especially the younger generation.

Then I met another man at church. Let's call him Bob. I was attending services and meeting with the recovery group. I was beginning to straighten out my life and become a more stable and balanced man. This new path allowed me to meet many good people, including Bob and his family. Bob and I got along well, and he slowly became a mentor for me in several areas. He taught me about manhood, by example. I learned from him about controlling my anger. He advised me on how to make better life decisions. One day, Bob and I were talking about life, daily stress, and his family. We got on the subject of his business, and he casually mentioned that he was looking to hire a new salesperson. He asked me if I was any good at that kind of work. I thought, *yeah, I could sell any sort of illicit drug you want me to, bro!* But I didn't say that. Instead, I told Bob I had never tried sales before, but I imagined I would be pretty good at it. Clearly, my confidence was increasing.

Bob decided to give me a shot. I would need to go through their formal interview process, which included an application, a background check, and drug testing. Bob wanted to hire me, but we still had to fulfill all of the corporate procedures. I was excited about the opportunity, but then remembered that I had a criminal record. I would need to disclose that. There are so many things I wish I hadn't done. These are permanently on my record forever; those choices I made as a teenager and young adult will follow me for a lifetime.

I had a choice. I could give up the job opportunity because of my criminal past, or I could be optimistic, trust Bob, and take a chance. Being optimistic is another important principle in the My Warrior's Way. I had to have a positive outlook in that moment of my life. So that's what I did. I was honest with him and shared my truth, knowing I would accept the outcome.

We talked about it and Bob said, "Let's just see how it goes."

Of course, my criminal record did come up. Bob was eventually able to get me cleared for hire, as it had been a few years since the arrests. Looking back, I'm very glad that I chose to disclose it up front and be honest with him about the situation, instead of hoping, unrealistically, that it wouldn't come up. I have learned that it is important to get to know key people in your life really well at a deeper level. There are moments in any relationship when we must step out of our comfort zone and simply trust a person. I trusted Bob with my personal and confidential information, and in turn, he trusted that I had turned my life around for good. Bob saw something in me. He suspected that I had some talent for sales, and he offered me the job. It all came out of nowhere—as I have found that there are a lot of things to do in life when you have your radar turned on. I firmly believe that it was my new, more optimistic approach to life that created this career opportunity. Just like the man in *Trauma: Life in the ER*, I had a choice about how to approach my life and its challenges. Months earlier, I made a conscious decision to be positive and come from a mindset of abundance rather

DON'T HIDE. DON'T COMPROMISE.

than scarcity. My new sales job was in the steel industry. I called on construction companies. It was a field position, and the gig came with a company truck, gas card, a phone, and a laptop. I also received a great starting pay with benefits! And I even took up golf because that is a great way to close a big sale.

Everything was starting to come together. After a long six-year battle, I finally won full and complete custody of Ana. Her grandparents were a tremendous help in our adjustment to one another before taking her permanently. So even though I could have taken her a year earlier, I wanted to continue going back and forth to build a relationship with her where she could learn to be comfortable around me. Beforehand, it was all so toxic in the environment in her mother's apartment. Her grandparents helped me build that relationship with her. That fight was worth every second. I could have gone with every excuse to just give up. *She doesn't like me or want me.* I used everything I had, even financially. The custody lawyer I hired was close to $15,000 and I was only bringing in about $30,000 a year at that point. I didn't have a penny in the bank, but damn it, I am going to be her dad! I was living paycheck to paycheck, but I was determined. At the time, other than being a pre-teen leader, I still had little insight on what it was like to be a full-time father. I hadn't even been baptized a year yet; I was doing all the right things to prepare for my daughter to live with us. I had so much still to learn and so much growing up to do. But in hindsight, I was being her dad the moment those results were known. Parents, whether mothers or fathers, will fight and protect their children. Although I was young-minded and immature in many areas, in my heart I knew she was worth every ounce of goodness from me.

I was at the Shell gas station on Ventura Blvd, and Ana was in the car with me. Staring into my child's beautiful and innocent eyes, with strands of hair falling freely in her face, I told her how I felt. "I would like you to stay with me from now on. Forever." I remember that big smile on her face, and that slightly confused look. She was starting to connect with me a little bit. We had moments where she was relaxed and able to be my daughter. I shared a little more of the story. "Well actually, that's what's going to happen. You are going to stay here from now on. We are going to go back and get some of your stuff and then you will be with me forever." And that's what we did. She packed a suitcase and came to California, and we started our new life together as father and daughter, living under one roof. We now were a family of three.

Ana is my first hero and my first unconditional true love. She was just a child. My first superhero was a tiny little girl. Imagine that? She taught me the importance of responsibility and the incredible effort it takes to fight. No matter how long it would take, nothing was going to stop me from pursuing the only thing that mattered in my life. I was 29 years old and ready to be a father to my 9-year-old daughter.

Jason and Ana at Christmas,
Los Angeles, California, 2011

Ana is so beautiful, so smart, hard-working, with a very nurturing heart. My courageous daughter has had to endure many challenges in her young life and has had to take on the ones I haven't yet healed from. As each obstacle comes up, she fights through it and overcomes it. She has learned to become a loving individual who is still finding her way as she grows into a woman herself. Ana is the reason that I sit here today: a more stable and balanced man on a positive journey in life. She gave me purpose — to fight and love my real-life princess and to be her father. If I need some inspiration, I only have to think about her story, and how grateful I am to be in it. At the end of the day, you know what we all want most? To be truly loved, no matter what.

From that day forward, my daughter's love for me began to grow. It was gradual at first, but we were on to something. We both knew that deep down we wanted and needed each other. I wanted my daughter and needed her, and I could sense she secretly knew that she wanted me. The fight in me for her was no question. My no-quit rule comes from her. I've never quit on her, and I never will. I won the battle for her in the court system. The judge told me upon making the judgment that she was proud of the efforts I made over those six years and that she can't remember a case where a father fought so long and hard for a child. Man, did that feel so good to hear. But now, how do I win her trust and ultimately her heart? How do I father her? I'd give anything to have had a magic wand to heal all my hurts and given everything I needed to raise a secure, confident, and trusting young woman. I didn't know what I was doing and was just starting to learn how to be a good man myself. I honestly didn't know how to raise a little girl. It was a lot of pressure, and I didn't know how to do much, so I dove headfirst into the Bible and did what some of the other church dads were doing. I needed to learn, and I needed to learn fast. I was so afraid of her messing up that I became way too strict and overbearing. I didn't want her to end up like me or her biological mother. Instead of parenting her with unconditional love, I was parenting her with a worst-case scenario mindset, correcting her every move, our parenting was just so negative at that time. Remember, I had no healthy parenting or any parenting at all in that matter – and with no protection. I had been there and done that, and I didn't want my innocent daughter to walk the same path. The pendulum had swung. I wanted to guard and protect her but didn't know how to do that. I started checking her left and right. I was learning how to recover from all kinds of abuse and trauma myself. I kind of took those hardcore lessons on how to get sober from the chemical recovery classes and from my church leadership and applied them to my parenting.

Because my beautiful little girl came from trauma and an addict mother, I applied those same disciplines on her. The type of training I was getting was working for me and the other addicts, but she was a child. She needed love, support, and safety; not rules and restrictions. I couldn't make those distinctions at that time because of the complexities in raising a child, and still a young man in recovery myself. Vanessa lived with her parents and grandparents, and they were always together and loved each other very much. She was taken care of, and she came from a strict upbringing. So with the two of us, we were doubly strict.

With church, everything was transactional. If you do something wrong enough times, you have to earn your way back to righteousness and love. It was almost like an earned behavior. And if you couldn't get it together and follow exactly what was advised or taught, you were considered prideful, lost, and perhaps going to hell. Well, something like that. The church had a way of constantly reminding you of your sins and your weakness. We were never going to be good enough. The God I was learning about at this church was never going to be pleased with us. I adopted the same mindset with my precious new princess. I made the mistake of transferring that energy of what *isn't* right with her and added fear to go with it. Not a good combo at all. I have so many regrets. I wish I was able to show her how valuable she was to me in those early years. The problem was I didn't believe I was valuable, so how in the world could I give that feeling back to her?

As I reflect on our time together in the beginning, I know somehow my wounds have hurt her and shaped her to some degree. Even though I wish I could go back and re-do certain things, I don't regret the fun times we created as a family. I was a fun, silly, energetic girl dad, and we had a lot of laughs and good times together. Considering the cards I was dealt, I did my best; but unfortunately, my best was not near good enough. All I can do now is forgive myself, which is the hardest thing to do, but I must. Who do I need to be for this now beautiful adult woman in order for her to count on me and know that I am her safe place? Being a dad is not just 18 years of your kid's life. It's a lifetime, and I am committed to becoming a better and better dad each and every day for the rest of my life to my Ana bear. To all my fellas who grew up without this male guidance and have a daughter or daughters, I beg you to do the self-work. We must raise and continue to affirm our girls to know their worth and become secure in receiving real love. It starts with your willingness to mend what you have now and start healing yourself.

One weekend, Vanessa and I decided to attend a Landmark seminar, which is a self-help realization conference. So much truth was revealed to both of us that weekend. We gained enough courage to be honest in how we both felt about our marriage. Mostly, it was me stepping into full transparency and Vanessa holding space where her ego was not involved. It was one of those powerful weekends that would quake my foundation but was necessary for responsibility and growth. We got woke. There is no freedom if there is no truth.

Inspiration was in full gear like never before. We all find inspiration in different ways. Being inspired is another essential way of being when it comes to living your Warrior's Way. I needed this. We all do. One common thread is that most people love to see someone overcome extreme challenges. Who doesn't love a superhero or a figure like Mother Teresa? There is a famous TED Talk bit by Steve Jobs called, "How to Live

Before You Die." He gave this talk to students at Harvard, even though he was a college dropout. He was a fatherless boy who was adopted by strangers. He took big risks and made countless mistakes. But he ended up changing the world. People like that inspire me.

I sometimes think about his day-to-day life, what it must have felt like to fail so often and so publicly. He started in that garage with Steve Wozniak, both of them facing rejection after rejection. Those who were supposed to love him had abandoned him. He had every reason not to trust people and not to even try to do something great. But despite everything that got in the way, he kept getting back up, trying newer and more innovative techniques. He went on to change the world. This is why movies like *Braveheart, Gladiator,* and *Forrest Gump* have so much appeal. The heroes in these movies face real challenges, even risking death. In the process of overcoming them, they realize their true potential. In *Gladiator,* the fighter, Maximus, was betrayed and lost everything he loved. He was extremely discouraged—but not defeated. He got back up and fought for what was right until his very last breath. Inspiration is contagious and attractive. When I realized this, I became and remain inspired by those around me who'd become warriors themselves.

On the flip side to that, it can be scary, too. We can be so stuck in our own mud; we really need the words and actions of others spurring us along to remember who we truly are. I was inspired that weekend to be authentic, honest, and brave. I needed someone to call me out on the ways I was hiding. Our marriage was never fully authentic, romantic, or passionate. We both can comfortably say that we weren't in love. We loved each other and felt the same way about a bunch of things, but we were never truly in love as husband and wife. We were conditioned to believe that divorce is a punishable sin leading to hell. I had no choice but to stay so focused on bettering our church roles, agendas, and raising our child. It was almost like a business partnership, but with partners who truly cared about each other and the welfare of others. I can say we were both selfless. So now what do we do?

*"The meaning of life is to find your gift.
The purpose of life is to give it away."*

—Pablo Picasso

CHAPTER 6
WOUNDED HEALER

We still didn't know what we were doing or how to come out of this. Our marriage was on the rocks, but we had hope. We went to counseling, and I also did individual counseling for years. We were open with our church friends who prayed for us. We really tried to make it all work.

Vanessa's heart always wanted to go on a mission trip and an opportunity in our church came up. Shortly after we attended the Landmark seminar, Vanessa, Ana (12 years old), and I boarded a plane headed to El Salvador. We were on a mission trip. Little did we know that it would change our lives in ways we never saw coming. Our team consisted of 11 people, on our way to visit our sister church in San

Salvador, which was part of the International Church of Christ. It was a dangerous time to go because the MS-13 Gang, also known as the Mara Salvatrucha, had taken over the country. The criminal gang originated in Los Angeles with intentions of protecting Salvadoran immigrants from other gangs in the area. They grew and by this time were international. They were robbing and bombing buses, and kidnappings and murders were happening daily. There was an 8:00 p.m. curfew enforced by the government. Now, why in the world would anyone think of going to El Salvador during these times, and taking their child with them? We both felt called to make this trip happen.

It was not the time to flash your threads and cool kicks. We didn't wear any jewelry, fancy clothes, or any name brands. It was so perilous that we had to hire two off-duty police officers armed with AK-47s to watch over us every day, from morning to night. We even saw one of the gang members go into a bus in front of us to collect cash from the driver. At that moment, I held up my phone to take a quick photo, but the armed guard grabbed my wrist to pull it down, telling me to stop. If the police officer had to cover that action, it was clear who was in control. It was crazy.

A tropical storm came in one evening and two other brothers from El Salvador were trying to pick up speakers for Church the next day. We were past curfew and had to drop one of them off. He insisted we let him off before heading into his neighborhood. There was a huge storm and we told him absolutely not. He said we would most likely get robbed and murdered if we came in. He walked miles in the hard rain and wind to get home. The next morning, there were floods and mudslides in the region and over 100 lives were lost. I'll never forget the hearts of those families.

At that time in El Salvador, you were either rich or poor. There really was no such thing as the middle class. Even those who didn't have much were so joyful and giving. They gave what they had. On a beautiful sunny day, we took a short trip to a village in the mountains in Suchitoto. The best thing happened when we arrived: the women had elotes (corn on a stick) ready for us to eat, along with atol de elote, which is a warm and creamy sweet corn drink.

We were there to assist and support and we ended up teaching them hygiene practices like brushing their teeth. We brought toothbrushes and toothpaste for them, and we gave them clothes and installed toilets in the school bathrooms. We also cleaned up the classrooms and pulled huge rocks out of the dirt to build a soccer field. After we created the soccer area, we ended up playing a game with the boys from the village. We were helping the kids and they all wanted to wrestle with me. They were laughing and calling me "The Hulk" in Spanish. As I was playing and messing around with them, I looked over at Vanessa and tears were streaming down her face.

"Seeing how those kids enjoy you and seeing how you enjoy those kids is amazing and beautiful," she later said to me.

Where are all these kids' dads? Most of their dads were in America trying to make money for their family. These kids were really loved, but they didn't have the guidance of a male figure. Boys crave approval and can receive tremendous confidence from strong caring men whether it's a preacher, mentor, or gang leader. If these voids are being met in one form or another, they will continue to follow that leader and path. Ultimately, they seek to be man enough for the world around them. This struck a loud chord with me and solidified a real moment that what I was doing was not just playing with kids. They knew they had my full attention. They were so happy, and afterward we took a photo flexing our 'guns' and laughing. They were hanging on me on every side. I was a human jungle gym. There were a few other men there that day as well, but the kids seemed to gravitate toward me. And man, did they make me feel like a million bucks! That's all I thought about throughout the rest of our trip. I couldn't stop thinking about all those beautiful kids, their laughter and smiles, and the way I felt being with them all day.

We really learned what it meant to truly live from the heart; nothing based on your bank account or the things you own. We were so thankful for that incredible experience and on the plane ride home, our time spent with them kept flashing through my head. Vanessa pulled up our photos from her digital camera and came upon the one she took in Suchitoto with the boys. It was something else! They were laughing and jumping all over me, having so much fun just being kids! I can still hear them yelling and laughing and loving every minute of it! Something happened to me in that instant. It all clicked. I turned to look at Vanessa and told her this was it. I wanted to help children without fathers. Her eyes danced with excitement as she smiled back big and wide, whispering the words I wanted to hear, "Yes, Jason. That's it." We both knew then that this was the beginning of a new path. We felt that we could make a difference in the lives of fatherless children. You see, up until that amazing encounter with those young boys, Vanessa and I shared ideas about how I could get involved with fatherless boys, specifically. I envisioned myself making a difference, but I just didn't know how it was going to happen. All I knew was that before the trip, I was in counseling and facing my fatherless wounds. I was digging into my pain and trauma. I wanted so badly to see the light at the end of the tunnel.

Jason in El Salvador, 2009

When we got home, I decided to seek out advice. I didn't want to make any rash or dumb decisions, so I talked to a few of the men who I fully trusted. One of them was the man who gave me my first sales job, Bob. I made an appointment with him, sat down, and laid out my initial plans. I spilled my guts. He saw the energy in my eyes. Guess what he said to me?

He leaned back in his chair and said, "Sounds like a really nice thing to do, but I just don't see anything like that working outside of a church setting. Sorry to lay it on you like that, Bro. But you asked me and that's my opinion."

Wow. What a discouraging response. It was especially hard coming from someone I trusted so much! I expected some support, and maybe a probing question or two to challenge my thinking. His response wasn't the approval I was looking for, and Bob didn't offer any constructive feedback for me. I got shut down. I took his summary blow-off with a grain of salt.

I walked away from this conversation a little dismayed, but not dissuaded.

My plans to launch were still in place. Later that week, I joined my good friend, Joe Buzzello, for a late afternoon round of golf at our private golf club. My career in sales was progressing very well. I advanced to another position in a different company. The income was solid enough for us to have a country club membership. I had taken up golf and Vanessa and I thought Ana would enjoy the pool and all the activities.

Joe Buzzello was an extremely successful businessperson. He built a large business unit for a Fortune 500 company in their Los Angeles market. People came to him for advice, and he seemed to enjoy contributing freely to their success. He loved mentoring—my kind of guy! The fact that we'd become golf buddies was an opportunity to pick his brain. Because Joe was such a fan of helping others grow, I was sure he'd 'get' what I wanted to do. I was extremely excited to tell him all about the idea so that he could give me two thumbs up. I guess that's what I really wanted—blind validation. But Joe didn't give that to me. As we made our way around the East Course at Braemar Country Club in Tarzana, California, he listened intently to my plans. He asked me some good questions—a lot of questions; questions nobody else had asked. I soon figured out that he had some reservations. He held his opinion back for a long time until I finally pushed him for his feedback.

He took a deep breath and said, "Jason, I like your heart and I like your idea, but I don't think you should launch this organization the way you have it planned. I love the passion you have for it, and I believe that it would be an awesome resource for communities across America. But I'm feeling like there may be too much risk for you and your family. I would like to see you prove the model first without walking away from your main source of income."

His answer broke my concentration. My immediate thoughts and emotions were, *What the hell, Joe! I thought you were one of the smartest dudes I know. Maybe you're just another idiot who doesn't get this really great thing that's lighting up my heart and mind. And damn it... I missed that easy putt!*

Looking back a few years later, I came to understand what Joe was really trying to tell me. He wanted me to create a well-written plan, start with a smaller test pilot model, and perhaps seek a modest amount of outside funding instead of personally taking on all of the risks. He was trying to guide me toward a more patient and pragmatic way of thinking. I was looking for validation, and when I didn't get that, all I heard was, "Jason, you're as stupid as that idea."

I also had another brilliant well-educated friend named Jeremy Vandervoet who would meet with me sometimes weekly to guide me on how to go about things and see things through the lens of business. I could sense his frustration with me because I didn't know what I was doing. It took a lot of explaining for me to understand many things. It was like learning a new language, but it didn't stop him from helping me. He was a patient teacher. Jeremy was my good friend, and we had a lot of laughs. He helped me so much, all while still knowing I was definitely in over my head. He knew I was too stubborn and there was probably no stopping me. He stuck in there, and I am grateful for him.

I'd fought so hard not to be that dumb kid from Ohio anymore. Because of that, I didn't deal with rejection very well. At the time, I couldn't recognize this. I still had some insecurity and immaturity about me. I was still learning—and I expect I always will be. I also discussed my idea with a few others who all had Joe's similar concerns.

So, guess what I did? I ignored all the smart people I'd sought out for input and launched my organization. It was something I *knew* God was calling me to. It was the first time I genuinely trusted my gut on something that other, smarter people advised me against. I have learned many lessons in my life, and I know there are many more to come. But here's one I don't want you to miss. *Sometimes, you just have to trust your gut.* You must be willing to put yourself out there, even if you might fail, even if you might wind up being wrong, because you know in your heart that it's right for you to take that step and move forward.

What I am about to say is very important. The reason I knew this had to happen was that deep down in my soul, the spirit of God was guiding me. He put that dream in my heart and chose me. I have learned that I was chosen before I was born. I had to go through all the hard stuff because humanity needed me to awaken. "Jason, you are doing this, but you are not going to be alone." I tell you, just like a navy seal must go through intense training I, too, had to go through some vigorous battles for the mission. Preparing for this was brutal and painful. And I believe with all my heart that the spirit of God was giving me the ultimate training, getting me ready, and He knew I needed it. Here is 1 Chronicles 28:20-21 that solidified my beliefs:

20 *David also said to Solomon his son, "Be strong and courageous, and do the work. Do not be afraid or discouraged, for the Lord God, my God, is with you. He will not fail you or forsake you until all the work for the service of the temple of the Lord is finished.* **21** *The divisions of the priests and Levites are ready for all the work on the temple of God, and every willing person skilled in any craft will help you in all the work. The officials and all the people will obey your every command."*

I knew that He was calling me to do the work and signaling me to go for it. After getting Vanessa's approval, we would end up investing our entire savings, all the money we worked so hard to earn, into our project.

Brené Brown says that "Faith is a place of mystery, where we find the courage to believe in what we cannot see and the strength to let go of our fear of uncertainty."

That is the place I felt this calling from. I was willing to risk all of it for what I believed was going to be my life's work. I was all in. I've learned that it's perfectly okay if others don't understand or approve. Sometimes you must be *willing to risk being wrong* and look like an idiot; but that's okay. I was ready to do this. Mind you, I came from the gutter. What did I have to lose?

It's been fifteen years since that golf course conversation with Joe Buzzello. Ironically, Joe is involved in the writing of this book. He's been truly instrumental and supportive. He's helping me structure both the book and the new training curriculum we are launching. Joe is an amazing man—even if he's been wrong a few times. Kidding aside, I've asked Joe for his advice many times over the last fifteen years, and his feedback has always been valuable. However, that day it wasn't what I wanted to hear, and it wasn't going to stop me. Joe has also taught me, "You never make a right decision. You make a decision, then you work like hell to make it right." God puts some great opportunities in front of us if we're looking for them. That's who Joe Buzzello is. He's a good-hearted man. And that's what friendship really is, right? Being willing to put your heart and soul and trust in someone else. It's okay if you don't always agree on everything. You shouldn't even want a friend or acquaintance who says yes to all of your ideas. Friends who challenge you in a caring manner are critical in your life. Despite Joe's careful and loving admonitions, I still decided to dive into the deep end and form Young Warriors. I committed all my time and financial resources in starting the organization. My vision was big, and my passion was bigger.

Everything about our lives changed. After all that we saw and experienced, we altered our spending habits. I canceled my membership at the country club, Vanessa canceled her Equinox membership, and we started by helping people in El Salvador get through college. I quit my solid business sales job making a six-figure income to start a nonprofit with no experience or real plan. Talk about risking it all, we did just that. Of course, we reached a point where our money did run out. We went from living in a 3,300 square foot home and driving a custom Audi to giving it all up and eventually needing government assistance. I wasn't afraid of it, though, because I had been there before. That is how invested we were. We were not giving up. Money cannot buy happiness and peace. Sure, it can buy cool things and even fun times, but that doesn't bring long-lasting peace or happiness to your heart and soul. For me, I am happier now with less stuff. After our trip, I made a choice to not be money-driven; instead, be driven to give, heal hearts, and help other hurting people. I had a successful ten-year business career and made it from rags to riches and now heading back from riches to rags. Well not, wealthy rich, but for me and where I come from, that was riches. I think you get what I am saying. In hindsight, I know now that God had and continues to have my back, because I heard His call and responded. I acknowledge that that is what He put in my heart to do with my life. I listened to my new 'dad' and now we're in the same business. Here is what I mean.

"Pure religion undefiled before God and the father, is this: To help the fatherless and widows in their affliction." JAMES 1:27

"A father to the fatherless, a defender of widows is God in His holy dwelling." PS 68:5

I was chosen to do this. We had plans to serve the youth on a larger scale. Vanessa supported me in every way. Young Warriors was born— to be a voice for the fatherless. I had no business background and no high school diploma; just a true, unmitigated desire to see change in our fatherless homes. I was determined to somehow figure it out. I had a new dream that was going to be a reality: **The Young Warriors Foundation.**

Working on pure excitement and adrenaline, I introduced the program first within our church. I knew some families without a father. Again, at the time we were working with the youth ministry and saw some deep needs. These single moms were holding it down but could use some support. A few other men in the church became mentors and there we were – meeting with these fatherless boys and bonding. The desire to get this nonprofit off the ground grew by leaps and bounds.

One young boy won my heart, his name is Shaolin Wonder Smith. Wonder is now a handsome, talented, and caring young man who was offered a contract to play professional basketball in Germany. Because of covid, travel issues, and timing, his plans changed. He is now learning business and consulting. We are incredibly proud and excited for him. He was the first ever Young Warrior. Wonder's mom, Ashley, is one of the most amazingly resourceful people I have ever met. A single mom of two great kids, Wonder and Macchiati, I've seen her put her children first at every single turn, before anything and everything else in her life. Though Ashley has had various health problems, she never let that stop her from making every effort to raise her children as balanced, healthy, and happy young people. Like many single moms, her resources were limited. If she didn't have a car, she still found a way to get the kids to their sporting events, to every birthday party, and to church every Sunday. She got them into a great private school on full scholarships.

She sent them to camps and on field trips that most kids with just one parent wouldn't be able to go to. All of this was possible because she identified the resources available to her and used them, better than most single moms I know. Many of those resources were the people in her life and her kids' lives. She would reach out to other moms and people from church—even to me or other mentors in her kids' lives.

I can picture Ashley now: sweating, running around, and making calls to make it all work. Whether it was a ride or financial assistance, she made it happen. She was dealt a tough hand, like many of us. But that never stopped her because it was never about her—it was about her children. Following Ashley's example, I am never ashamed to ask for help or funding for my Young Warriors. It's not about me—I'm just a voice for boys who don't have a voice. When you live for something bigger than yourself, you are able to ask without shame and receive without guilt.

Jason and Wonder, Santa Monica, California, 2008

My office was in a closet in our two-bedroom apartment for the time being. We began to go on a serious budget to make this happen. Leo had a business and said I could use his office for Young Warriors. It was down the street from Galpin Ford in the San Fernando Valley. One day I decided to contact them to see if they wanted to help kids without dads. I walked in there one sunny afternoon and Carolynn, the secretary, took down my information. She handed me a card. I called the number on the card the following week. I didn't hear anything back. Still persistent, I stopped by one late afternoon and was able to meet with the CEO of Galpin Motors, Brad Boeckmann. The man is incredibly special and sincere. I began my conversation by thanking him for meeting with me.

He offered me a seat in his office and began the conversation. "I am impressed by your persistence. And I like what you're trying to do. That's honest work." He took a minute to let that sink in with me. "Now explain to me what you are trying to do."

At that point, his secretary, Carolynn, told him that I was genuinely trying to help these kids. I shared from my heart about our crisis of fatherless children. We had a great conversation, and he cut a check to the Young Warriors for $1,000 at that very meeting. I was very encouraged. It was our first corporate donation. Other than Vanessa, me, and a few others from church, someone else finally believed in the idea. From then on, Galpin Motors was in and partnered with Young Warriors. That relationship continued with hosting small events for our nonprofit, and two years later Galpin Motors sponsored us with a $15,000 check and then helped us purchase a 15-passenger van to take the Young Warriors on fun field trips. That's when things really began to happen. I will spend the rest of my life helping boys who don't have fathers by teaching, guiding, and inspiring them. I wanted to help the boys become productive and respected young adults in our community. I wanted to offer fatherless boys encouragement, care, and positive mindsets to model and emulate. I had no idea how or when this could or would happen. I wasn't sure what shape it would take or what the program would look or feel like. However, through prayer, meditation, planning, and conversations, our current Young Warriors foundational structure took life. It helped that I was optimistic about my plan.

I expected everyone else around me to have the same passion and vision as I did. I anticipated that everyone in my universe would invest the same effort as me. My naiveté led to discouragement and frustration. I felt like I was being let down left and right, even by some of my closest friends. Eventually, I realized that people have busy schedules and their own priorities. It's not that they didn't care, but they had their own families, job priorities, and lives. The time wasn't there. I had to swallow another hard lesson. I soon accepted that this was my decision and my battle.

In a nonprofit organization, the Board of Directors is key to making the organization grow and succeed. I have had a few of the wealthiest, most successful, and influential people look at me squarely in the eye and tell me they were all in. My disappointment came when a few months later, my calls and emails to these same people went unanswered. Some of them simply disappeared.

Of course, this was tremendously discouraging to me at first. I wondered how they could let my boys down. I trusted them. It hurt because I knew that I couldn't build this organization alone. I knew that I didn't have the skillset that some of these men and women had. But this was my vision and my calling — not theirs. So, I learned that no matter how rich, successful, or influential somebody is, if their actions do not benefit the boys in my program, I simply say *no thank you*. I must be a relentless leader, and I cannot expect anyone else to be as relentless as me. So here I was, a high school dropout attempting to

Brad Boeckmann, Galpin Ford, Los Angeles, 2009

start and run a foundation to help children understand that they are not alone. Ironically, I was trying to do things alone. Go figure. But hey, that was my choice, and I was all for the cause. I wanted to help boys just like me when I was young. There was yet another lesson for me to learn. I discovered that one of the most difficult factors when you have honestly and passionately changed your own life is the realization that not everyone wants to change theirs. They may even speak the language of change, but their actions don't line up. Regardless, I had to carry on and so I gave it everything I had. To begin with, a guy by the name of Louis believed in our program and took an interest in what we were trying to grow. He was our first program director. I don't know what I would have done without him. This amazing man is truly a gift—he backed my vision and was all in. I guess you could say he had faith in me and where we were headed.

One other huge part to all of this was that I needed to be optimistic and believe deep in my heart that I was going to give it my all, *no matter what.* I'm not a naturally optimistic person, and I'm still learning to become one. In fact, I was raised to worry about almost everything.

Because of my difficult childhood, I adopted a distressing and gloomy outlook. I brought negativity, worry, and doubt to every situation. As my young life progressed, I tried to fight off these demons. I found that the more I strove to improve the quality of my thoughts and actions, the more often I won those battles.

There was an episode of the reality show *Trauma: Life in the ER* that I watched which really struck me. It featured a man who had just lost both his arms from the shoulders down. He talked about his life, and he seemed genuinely grateful. He spoke about his family and how grateful he was to have his legs and his ability to see and smell and hear. It was hard for me to understand how he could get over the devastating facts of his condition. He had just lost both of his arms from his shoulders down and wasn't destroyed spiritually or emotionally. That's a mindset to strive for. I remind myself every day that it's my choice how I view each situation, whether I choose a positive outlook or a negative one. Either perspective can become my truth, and the choice is mine.

Vanessa and I are proud of what has become of the Young Warriors. Our foundation has done more than both of us could have ever dreamed. When I think about the time we were together in our marriage, I focus on all the great things we achieved. Optimism is a cornerstone of our Young Warriors program because we both had it. I finally gained an optimistic outlook about the direction of my life.

You know who can really teach you about finding the good in others? Children. They are authentically pure and present. Imaginations bigger than skyscrapers. Their minds have no limits, nothing is holding them back. Their little brains aren't concerned about what the critics think. They are so fixated on the magic of a balloon or running and feeling the grass under their feet. They truly are our greatest gift. Watch them and you will learn from them. They have always been who I admire the most. They are honest with how they are feeling, good or bad. No forced filters. If they see something they don't like or love, they will tell you. Before they are tainted by the world, they are trusting, loving, and caring. I see them as my little superheroes. They keep me feeling and acting young at heart. Being with kids has always been my safe place. When I am with them, I feel a transcending peace that teaches me how to be present and in the moment. They are our future, and how we choose to love them will soon become the shape of humanity. Honestly, all of us should be paying attention and spending quality time with them. Once they grow up a bit, they will experience some hits, and they will need us to support and guide them.

And what if that kid or young man or adult comes from unfair circumstances? What starts happening to his heart? It becomes hard for him to survive, especially, without a positive male role model in his home. Young warriors enroll in our program around the age of nine or ten. There are some heartbreaking stories in their lives. Some have been molested and beaten, and many are clearly hurting inside. All their fathers have left them in some way. We gather together in small groups each week to talk about things they are going through. We don't correct them, and we don't tell them how to feel, we stand beside them. Throughout the program we are constantly working on their perspective of life. By the end of the year, each child winds up sharing positive aspects of something that they previously viewed in a negative way. We help them slowly form a different long-term view, a more positive and hopeful outlook on their situation and the world. No matter what they have been through, having an optimistic mind is key to their success. And even though they may have wounds, trauma, and are often abandoned when they come into the Young Warriors program, there is a healing process that happens.

I created Young Warriors to be a safe place for these boys. They are taught how to deal with the wounds of their heart and pains that are deep. They learn to work hard and play hard. Working hard and giving your all comes before play. As they grow, they become young warriors and they realize the truth. That is, they are prized and worth more than they ever thought possible. We give them a warrior vision. One of strength, confidence, and love. We don't just send them on their way. We stay with them as they grow from children to teens and adults. Just as a father would be, we are the warrior's family for life.

However, at the time, as life would have it, I was thrown another curveball. While everything was new and scary and inspiring, and we were on our way to building our foundation, I got some devastating news about my baby sister.

*Young Warriors at Grant Elementary School,
East Hollywood, California, 2015*

"Goals live on the other side of obstacles and challenges. Be relentless in pursuit of those goals, especially in the face of obstacles. Along the way, make no excuses and place no blame."

—Ray Bourque

CHAPTER 7
PLEASE, GOD, NO

Amanda had significant struggles with drug abuse and managing her life. She said she wanted to change, and I know deep in her heart she really did want that. My sister was a beautiful, loving, and caring woman, but she couldn't seem to take action to overcome her situation. I remember times when she would call me from Ohio hysterically crying, saying she was finally ready to change her life.

She told me, "I'm ready to stop using, I want to be better for my kids, and I can't do it here. Can I come live with you?"

While we were on the phone, her new husband walked into the

room, and she dropped the phone on her lap while I was still on the line. He was aggressive toward her and snarled with contempt. "Who the hell are you talking to?"

He was listening from the other room and started going off on her. He was yelling vicious obscenities and tearing her apart with his words. He was verbally crushing my baby sister, telling her she was nothing but a whore among other things. It was heartbreaking. I was in California unable to do anything to help my sister. My baby sister was living a nightmare. One famous quote I have revised is sticks and stones may break your bones, but words can absolutely destroy you. And my baby sister was crushed. Within an hour, I purchased a plane ticket for her. I told her I would take care of her as long as she made an effort to get clean. I was going to help her get set up with a healthy living situation and environment and have the kids move with her to California. It would be a new start for everyone. When the day came for Amanda to board the flight, I couldn't reach her. She was nowhere to be found.

My baby sister was using again. The pains in my heart were unbearable. I needed to understand her. I discovered a book written by Gabor Mate titled, *In the Realm of Hungry Ghosts*. It helped me so much. My sister was hurting so deeply. I recommend this book to anyone caught up in a situation where a friend or relative is using heroin or any drug and there is a desire to understand how to care for their loved ones, as well as understand themselves better. Week after week the calls increased. I was beginning to worry. Then I got a call from my cousin, who never calls, saying Amanda was in really bad shape, and that she had never seen her like that before. She said she was on the verge of losing her kids and that somebody needed to do something or else she would. I called Amanda and she was very high. I knew then, after that conversation that Child

Protective Services was in touch with her. I told her she had two choices. She can let the government take the kids or I can take them. My sister begrudgingly said okay. She put them first because deep down she knew this was the best choice. You see, Amanda and I had always wished we would have been adopted or had a safer childhood. My nephew was eight and my niece was old enough to make her own decision, so at the time she did not want to make the move. Will, on the other hand, seemed very excited to come to California and stay with his big fun uncle. Vanessa and I discussed it, and we didn't give it a second thought. Times like those, I think about what it would have been like if someone would have done that for me.

I booked a red-eye flight the next night and rented a car. Our return flight was booked for the following day. I called her to say I was on my way. She didn't want me to come to her house because it was a drug house. She was going to meet me at the corner of where she lived. I called to let her know I was there. A couple of minutes later, I could see my nephew with his tiny little kid suitcase. I also saw my sister stumbling her way toward me. She was so high on heroin, she couldn't talk. I had never seen Amanda like this before. There was a time when she was so beautiful and radiated such a warmth that everyone wanted to be around her. Now she was skinny, strung out, and had gaping holes in her arms. It was heartbreaking. I gave my sister a really tight hug and told her I loved her very, very much. She gave her son a kiss and told him it was going to be good for him. She had tears streaming down her face. My baby sister was brave. She grew up in this same environment. Love can look all kinds of ways and ways that may not even make sense. She loved her son and daughter immensely. Sometimes love means letting go but never leaving them. I reached down for Willy's hand as he got into the car. I couldn't control my emotions. I was sobbing so hard. I turned around to him in the backseat and said I was sorry for crying like this. He looked at me... so lost. I asked him if he had any idea why I was crying.

He said, "She's fine. She's always like that." He wasn't connected. He had no idea, so I shifted the conversation.

"Are you hungry? You could have anything you want."

He said he wanted McDonalds.

We got a hotel room in Cleveland with two queen beds. He was happy jumping up and down on them. We went to the jacuzzi, and he loved that too. I was exhausted, but he was having a great time. We went to a restaurant, and he called it a fancy dinner. I was still so broken over my sister, and it took everything I had to not show my emotions to this innocent child. It was his first time in a hotel and on an airplane. Little Willy was eight years old and the most joyful and loving kid a parent could want.

When he met Ana and Auntie Nessie, without saying a word and with a beautiful smile on his face, he handed each of them a straw he took from the airport restaurant. It was his gift to them. I remember he came with one suitcase containing his belongings, and all the clothes smelled like an ashtray full of cigarette butts. He wore baggy pants and a big shirt. That day we went to Old Navy and bought him a new wardrobe, pajamas, and shoes. Ana and Willy immediately loved each other. I remember them running in the furniture store, so happy as they picked out their new bunk beds, because now we were a family of four. Then we were off to Panda Express, which is Willy's favorite to this day. We were excited, nervous, and scared, all at the same time; but knew we would figure it out. A blended family has its own rewards and hardships, as long as the intention comes from pure love. Both kids rewarded us in ways we could never describe. They were, by far, our biggest and most influential teachers. Will is now an adult, full of intelligence, creativity, and kindness. Ana reminds us every day how lucky we are to have her in our life. She, too, is smart, caring, witty, generous, loving, and almost as hilarious as her father (me, haha). We are so proud of all that she has overcome in her life and who she is becoming. Our 25-year-old daughter considers and calls Vanessa her mother, even though there is not a biological connection. Both are proud of the deep bond they have for each other. Which says a lot, because I have learned that good mother/daughter bonds are hard to come by. But theirs? It may be the most beautiful relationship I have ever witnessed.

Jason (left) Will 8 years old
Santa Monica Mountains, California

So there we were, now a blended family of four and running this non-profit. What an adventure. Over the years, I worked hard to surround myself with people who had education and gifts that I didn't yet possess. I was now CEO of a nonprofit organization, yet I only had a tenth-grade education. I learned to swallow my pride, admit there were things I didn't know, and reach out for help. I now have someone who I reach out to for help with our corporate finances, accounting, child development strategies, copywriting, and so much more. I found other professionals who are willing to help me manage issues such as employees and volunteers. I found that the more resources I use, the less frustrated I get.

Chill, our dog (left), Ana, Vanessa, Jason, Will (right)
Encino, California, 2010

We all have the ability to inspire another. Maybe it's just me, but I think men especially tend to want to be someone's hero. Deep down inside, we feel like we can become that. I think that's why certain movies appeal to men. When we learn how to inspire just one person, it can snowball. Who knows? We can end up inspiring hundreds, thousands, or even millions of people. But each of us must first start by inspiring one very important person: that inner you. Once I felt inspired by what I wanted to do with my life, I found mentors along the way who were willing to help me. I naturally wanted to pay forward what I had received. When I became focused on serving others, inspiring myself came naturally. Serving other people—especially kids who are hurting like I once was—fills my heart and spirit in a way that nothing else ever has.

As I was working on my childhood trauma at one of my sessions with a counselor, a great man named Mike Newman told me to go home and look at a picture of myself as a boy, and ask my then 10-year-old self this question: "What do you need?" I found this to be a very emotional experience, but I highly recommend it. The person I trusted most in this world as a boy was myself. Now as a grown man, that little boy, me, still struggles with trusting others. You know what that little boy told me? He told me he was afraid. He wanted to feel protected. He wanted his mom to stop drinking and doing drugs and he wanted her to spend time with him. He needed his mom. He wished she would come home because she had been gone for several days, and he missed her and was afraid. He wished she would spend less time partying with drunk men and take him somewhere fun. He told me he was sad and didn't have many friends.

Then he asked me a question that I couldn't answer. He asked me who his father was. It broke my heart for him, and for myself as a grown man. I told him, lovingly, that I still didn't know who his father was. I also said, *"If he knew who you were and who you are becoming, he would be so proud of you. He would lift you high up in the air and tell you how much he loves you. He would take you out to McDonald's, and to a movie and then spend the rest of his days with you, loving you as his beloved and beautiful son, Little Jason."*

When my adult self spoke those words to the photograph of my 10-year-old self, tears were streaming down my face and I felt my jaw tighten, holding back an anxious feeling of rage. But then I broke into the biggest and widest smile I managed in a long time. My eyes grew wide, and the tears stopped draining from my eyes. Looking at that photo of little Jason Hill, I gave a little snicker and said aloud, *"Hey, Buddy, you made it. But you're in for one hell of a ride."*

I felt proud of who I was. I was passing the hard knocks test growing up and every day I was learning more and more about myself. Things were beginning to fall into place. I gained the confidence to act on my idea for Young Warriors. I stayed relentless and persevered through my individual struggles.

In 2013, after Young Warriors had our first successful golf tournament to raise money, a mutual acquaintance of mine told former NFL Running Back Eric Dickerson about the foundation and set up a meeting for us to meet. Eric asked me about the foundation and why I was doing it. I took about thirty minutes and told him my life story. I wanted him to understand that it wasn't just a thing for me, it was my life's purpose. I believe he felt that. I then showed him and his wife, Penny, a video of what we do at the foundation. After he watched it, he told me a little bit of his story, and within minutes I could tell he was excited and willing to jump in and help. He said he loved the idea and could relate. We really hit it off and he was definitely feeling the cause. After meeting with Eric, we both decided to turn it into an annual Hall of Fame Golf Tournament, which still runs today. He wanted to use his celebrity status, contacts, and resources to help these boys believe that the underdog can also win. And win big. And here was my *1 Chronicles 28:20-21* scripture I mentioned earlier manifesting itself in front of me.

At a young age, Eric was in a similar situation to mine. He grew up without his biological father and mother. He was raised by his great-great aunt and went on to live an extraordinary life because of the choices he made. Eric was a skinny little boy who grew into a high school football star in Sealy, Texas. He went on to become one of the greatest college football stars ever while playing for his home state university, Southern Methodist University (SMU). But he didn't stop there. Eric entered the NFL in 1983 and was drafted second overall by the Los Angeles Rams—only behind the great quarterback, John Elway. As a running back for the Rams, he established the NFL's rookie rushing record of 1,808 yards, followed by a single-season 2,105 yards in 1984. Both records, and many more, still stand today. Eric spent a total of eleven seasons in the NFL playing for the Rams, the Oakland Raiders, Indianapolis Colts, and the Atlanta Falcons. Of course, I mean the incomparable NFL running back, Eric Dickerson. The same Eric Dickerson who was inducted into the NFL Hall of Fame in Canton, Ohio, in 1999. You should read his book, *Watch My Smoke*, because it is an amazing story of how he overcame and became the Hall of Fame man he is today.

When you read his football biography, you will understand all the obstacles and odds that were stacked against him. Eric grew up in a very small town with little opportunity. From an early age, he was hurt, used, lied to, stolen from, and disrespected. He got used to betrayal. The pressure of being in the national spotlight, as he was, would have taken many men out. Eric was incredibly misunderstood. Even through all that happened to him, he chose to become an example in many areas of his life. One particular area that stands out to me is that Eric is an incredible listener. He continues to give his heart, his time to those he cares about, and his money to others in need. It would have been very easy for him to push everyone away, to kick almost everyone out of his life because of the way he was treated. But Eric never did that. He taught me that no matter how many times you've been hurt, betrayed, lied to, stolen from, or doubted, there's always somebody out there who needs you to keep fighting. My friend, Eric, has one of the most relentless mindsets I've ever seen. He has also taught me about loyalty. He is one of the most loyal friends I've ever had. He just shoots it straight, good or bad, and I love it because I know he has my best interests in his heart and his great mind. He knows me so well, and I trust him deeply. It feels good to say that.

Growing up, I mistreated my girlfriend and other people I loved. Yes, I was raised horribly and felt like the whole world was against me. But I have learned through the battle as a warrior that all my poor decisions are still my responsibility. It's still on me to apologize, to prove my remorsefulness, and to try and make things right. A lesson I learned from Eric is that although you may get hurt, you must keep your heart *relentlessly* open to aligning with the right people. You never know what stranger may one day become the most important person in your life. And boy, was I going to need the resilience and inspiration for what was about to come.

Vanessa and I were very much unified in the nonprofit organization and loved these two beautiful children. It was her desire to homeschool both kids. It was scary at first, but they needed to know that we were there for them and committed to being in their lives every minute of

Jason (left), Eric Dickerson (right) and the Young Warriors

every day. They both came from traumatic living situations. Besides, the public school system was failing, bullying was high, and it was negatively affecting our daughter. We wanted them to experience structure, consistency, and love. Some of the other families in our church were doing it, so the social aspect of being with others their age was available and supported. Ana and Will were plugged in, and we all spent about three to four days a week doing something involved with our church. We were a solid foursome family, doing our best to live by God's words and always doing the right thing.

I felt so loved at first by the church, but years later I realized it was conditional. Don't get me wrong, people like Leo and a few others from the church gave me their love and friendship unconditionally. We had a strong committed community, but then I started to recognize more and more the agendas and conditions a member of the church had to abide by. I went from feeling loved by God to feeling afraid of God, which was weird because the better a Christian I became the more perfect I felt I had to be. I always felt guilty and afraid. Instead of knowing God as love, I knew Him as fear. It was terrible. I was starting to not feel it. The more I pulled away from it, the more Vanessa leaned in. We were beginning to feel the differences and tension between us. Part of the reason I stuck around in the church was that I had a wife who was very involved. My nephew liked going in the beginning, but my daughter didn't. Vanessa and I never really argued before, but now we did; it was usually over church and specific religious beliefs or church leadership tasks. We both felt the pressure to be perfect in God's eyes, whatever that meant. I felt like I was partially living a lie. Most of our marriage, we didn't argue or fight, but our arguments happened later on, and they had to do with our religious views. She was latching on more and more to the church, whereas, I was not interested anymore.

Religious beliefs can get in the way sometimes, and in our case it did. I simply didn't want to commit so strongly to our church, and Vanessa was not happy about that. We both knew it wasn't going to work. Yes, we gave it our best effort, but when it came down to it, I realized that I didn't want to stay in our marriage any longer. I'd 'hung in there' because I didn't want to make it about my selfish feelings. I was committed to doing the right thing for our kids and ourselves. I started to acknowledge how much the church was screwing up my family, especially my daughter. We faithfully and passionately followed rules and taught those rules over ten years to our children. I was starting to doubt everything. I didn't believe what I used to believe. I was becoming more and more convinced that staying together wasn't the right thing at all, for any of us. Not for me, not for Vanessa, and not for the kids. I was beginning to realize that I wanted the marriage to end, and I wanted to leave the church and their teachings. I was 40 years old. Ana was 18 at the time, and Will was 13.

Jason and Vanessa trying a donut before the divorce.

We tried everything. We talked to pastors, we confessed all our sins, confided in our close friends, and went to counseling for years. Finally, I made a difficult decision to separate and then divorce. When our church found out about it, they weren't happy. Looking back, when it came to the church leadership, it really wasn't about Vanessa and me at all. It never had been. They were far more concerned about doing things their way, and how our decision and the news would affect the other member of the church. At that time, Vanessa and I were part of the youth leadership team. We were a well-known couple within the organization. I understood their concern, but I was not thrilled with the way they responded to my decision. I knew the church's wrath was coming. In hindsight, I now believe that God didn't want us to get married all those years ago. Everything in my heart told me that at the time. God was trying to reach my heart, but I didn't let Him in. I simply wasn't tuned in. Yet, He still allowed it, and I believe it was for greater reasons; ones I for sure couldn't see at the time.

When we disclosed that we planned to divorce, it seemed crazy to our church. It didn't seem right to them. They were looking at us from the outside. The way I see it, trusting God truly means trusting Him fully, even when it might not seem right or smart to those you respect or admire. That is okay. Jesus had to trust his Father, God, his entire 33 years here on Earth, even though many thought he was crazy. These hard choices didn't seem right or easy. I lost friends I had for fifteen years or more, and some relationships were never the same again. Neither Vanessa nor I are still attending that particular church. After our divorce, we both decided to leave. In my opinion that church felt and acted more cult-like than any traditional Christian church I have attended before or after. Eventually, that drove me to seek spiritual fulfillment elsewhere. The church felt like a corporation with strict rules, which affected me and my views on God and Christ. I was young and vulnerable and a perfect tool to add to their daily recruiting numbers. I have since found out that this church's teachings had a history of destroying lives by manipulating the Bible to fit their agenda. It can be a struggle deciphering what are man-made rules and what are God's rules. Not everyone sees the scriptures the same way. It affected me so badly that it stunted my relationship with God.

The teachings I learned to live by scarred me and my family, mostly my already hurting innocent daughter and nephew.

I will say that there were some great people who attended and may still attend that church. Some of those people changed my life for the better, and I have nothing but love for them. I need to keep it real with you because being authentic and transparent is everything in a warrior's journey. I didn't know this at the time, but I was very hurt by both of these separations... with Vanessa and with the church. Deep relationships I had for years and years were gone. This was supposed to be my safe haven. The teachings really screwed me up. And they were from those I fully trusted. I realized many years later that I allowed myself to believe the same false narrative all over again. For me, being misunderstood equates to not belonging or being unlovable. I didn't stop to look at what was really going on with me on the inside. These people were my first real safe family and tribe. I think I was hurt from feeling misunderstood, and I just said screw it.

One afternoon I was in my driveway returning home from running an errand. I received a call from my mom's husband's sister. It was the worst way to hear bad news, especially from a person you don't want to hear it from. She reported, "Amanda is gone. Amanda died. They found her overdosed in her room at your mom's house. I'm at my son's basketball game. I can't talk long, but I just wanted you to know she died, and I am sorry."

It's a call no big brother should have to receive.. I fell to my knees in anguish. You see, Amanda was all I had. She was my family. My baby sister... gone. She was 35 when she passed. How can someone so young, so beautiful, and so loving, lose herself to heroin? My beautiful baby sister was found dead by my mom with a needle in her arm, while her abusive addicted husband lay next to her, passed out on Xanax. He died about a year later – also from a heroin overdose. Your first time, it is a choice. After that, it becomes a way of life in order to feel good and be functional.

I was in shock when I called Vanessa, hysterically crying and completely devastated. This was a difficult lesson. No matter how badly you want something for someone else and no matter what vision you have for them, you can't help them if they're not willing to take the necessary action.

Melody Beattie explains why it so pointless in trying to change other people's behavior:

"We cannot change people. Any attempts to control them are a delusion as well as an illusion. People will either resist our efforts or redouble their efforts to prove we can't control them."

I had never felt pain like this before. The more painful part was having to tell my 13-year-old nephew, Will, that his mother overdosed and was gone. He was in the middle of his Krav-Maga (military self-defense fighting) lesson when we got the news, and after practice Vanessa picked him up from his lesson and the two of them came to be with Ana and me. There were so many emotions going through my head; I didn't want to report such terrible news. I felt like I was going to crush his hopes and dreams. All he cared about was his momma. The whole point was for my sister to get better, get sober, and then he would go back to his mom. It's all he ever wanted. We were all together as a family, aching in our hearts. When Will heard my words, he just stared off into space, numbed out, and shut down. He didn't say a word. I saw him shrug his shoulders, and in the moment, there were no tears. He was so confused and didn't know how to apply this devastating news.

He finally said, "I kind of knew this day was going to come."

Sadly, I kind of knew, too; we both just hoped it wouldn't. How does a young boy process his own mother's loss and in the way she passed? Then Vanessa broke down. We were there as one, holding space and supporting him the best way we could. The last time he saw his mother was about two years prior to all of this.

We arrived in Ohio to attend the funeral. It was a very cold and dry winter day. Ice was everywhere and everything truly was dreary looking for a funeral. Most people in attendance looked like walking corpses, they were using meth and heroin. Addicts everywhere. It was sad to see how deep in my sister really was. It was like being at a rehab-intake.

Vanessa (left), Amanda (right)

Things were still the same back home. Nothing changed. During the ceremony, Will played the extended version of Amazing Grace on the violin in remembrance of his mom. Afterward, we went to this bar/hall for the reception. I was so sad that my baby sister was gone and so heartbroken for my nephew. I just wanted the day to end.

A few months after her passing, Will wanted to go back to Ohio. His father was getting released from prison, and he wanted to be with him. Our nephew was exhausted from it all, and understandably so. We agreed we would send him for the summer, but as it turned out, he ended up staying. It was his choice. My head was spinning, and my heart was slowly breaking... bit by bit. The family that I built, longed for, and had, was no more.

There was a lot of pain stirring up inside me. I slowly started going back to what I knew... women and alcohol. I was retreating back to those vices, but at the time I had no idea I was doing this. It was subconscious. I didn't deal with my grief, and at the same time I was trying to find my new way. It didn't take me long to meet someone who was everything I dreamed I could want. She told me she was going through a divorce herself, so of course we bonded and comforted each other. I was starting to really fall for her. She was sweet, beautiful, and sexy to me. We laughed so much together. We did everything and enjoyed each other's company. We dated for about 2 years and even got pregnant together but lost the baby along the way. That was hard for both of us; well... at least for me it was. She lived with her parents, and I kept asking to meet them and her family, but she would say it was too soon because her divorce wasn't finalized. Plus, her ex became close to her parents. That's sensible. I was the new guy, so I knew I had to be patient. After about a year, I finally met them at her college graduation, and it was great. Then she kept on delaying other smaller things and one time she disappeared for a few days. I was worried and thought something was wrong. I started to feel that something was off and began to not trust her. After about a two-year run, I told her it was best for us if we broke it all off because I knew in my gut that something just wasn't right. I really wanted to be with her and only her but had to call things off. She was upset and tearfully told me she couldn't see herself living without me. I had empathy but still had to officially call it off. It was interesting because with Vanessa I felt the intuition in my head. With this woman I felt it in my heart. We had a passionate physical connection. I came to realize I was "in lust" with her. Lust and love are siblings. Be careful with them, they can lead you down a slippery slope. All my undealt-with heartaches were just snowballing, and I was losing my footing. Little did I know that soon an avalanche was on its way.

"We have two lives, and the second begins
when we realize we only have one."

—Confucius

CHAPTER 8
YOU ONLY LIVE O̶N̶C̶E̶ TWICE

You never know what is coming next in your life. Even when you think you've worked enough on yourself, and you are growing to become a better person; you just don't know what's around the corner. Take it from me, when you feel like you have everything planned perfectly, things can and will come out of nowhere to test you, shape you, or break you.

On the early morning of September 15, 2017, I enrolled 30 new kids from 75th Street Elementary School in South Los Angeles, California. These 30 boys from South LA were selected for scholarships into our Young Warriors program. After that meeting, full of excitement, I walked across the street to meet with the head detective of the police department. He agreed to bring officers over to the schools to help mentor the kids. Talk about a great day! I was so happy, encouraged, and excited for our 30 new families. A friend of mine had a birthday that day, and we just had to celebrate all the victories. It was a perfect day to go out. We started with dinner and ten or so people, and we were having so much fun that a few of us decided to extend the evening at a late-night dance club in Santa Monica. Time passed quickly as I laughed it up with my friends and a few people we met. We were all having such a good time. Next thing I knew, I woke up in the Intensive Care Unit two weeks later strapped to my hospital bed. What the hell happened?

Story has it...

At closing time, my friends went outside to wait for our Uber, and I was following them. A man I didn't know – a complete stranger – ran up on me from behind and sucker punched me in the back of my head knocking me out — I was completely blindsided. He made contact so hard that I was knocked out in midair and fell on the concrete, fracturing my skull. Then he started kicking me in my ribs. My friends heard a commotion and jumped out of the car. The man ran back into the establishment as quickly as he had come out. It all happened so fast. My injuries were so severe that my friends didn't waste any time running after him. A firefighter who just happened to be driving by stopped to help. Someone called 911. The police report is frightening for me to read, but it's all I have to understand what actually happened to me that night.

I woke up in the Neuro ICU department at UCLA after spending two weeks in a coma. I looked around the hospital room, feeling completely disoriented. My body, arms, and hands were strapped down. My precious little daughter, Ana, had to keep stopping me from ripping the rest of the lines, wires, and sensors from my hands, arms, and head. I had breathing tubes and wires everywhere. The doctors would come in and ask me if I knew who I was, what year it was, and if I could remember the president's name. I couldn't remember anything. I had amnesia. I spent four weeks in the Intensive Care Unit getting tests after tests while they tried to stabilize my body.

I suffered a fractured skull and had several broken facial bones, including severe orbital and nasal breaks. My attacker broke five of my ribs, and I had a badly punctured lung. They had to put two tubes in my lungs so the blood could drain, and I could breathe. And if those injuries weren't bad enough, my vision was permanently damaged, and I sustained a severe traumatic brain injury (TBI). I couldn't remember anything for the better part of the next month after spending four weeks in the hospital. The brain is a fascinating organ, filled with billions and billions of neurons. It's an energetic and communicative instrument that speaks to our body. Tragically, my brain was unable to communicate with my body the way it did before all this happened. To this day I still can't take a very deep breath without feeling pain in my ribs and lungs. The gums and tooth area that were fractured are still numb. I lost hearing in my left ear. My eyesight has severely diminished from the permanent optic nerve damage. Because my head hit the concrete so hard it fractured my skull. I can't see clearly out of my right eye, as it is permanently damaged.

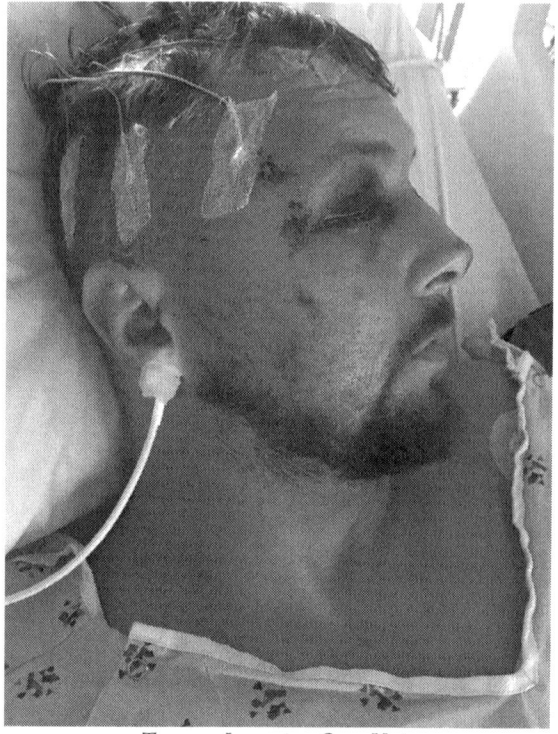

Trauma Intensive Care Unit
UCLA, 2017

I was using an alias witness-protection name because we had no idea who the man's identity was. Vanessa, by then my ex-wife, was by my side every day. She contacted my recent ex-girlfriend, and she came to help out daily, as well when I was in the hospital. I was too out of it at the time to know who was there. Vanessa was the queen bee and literally my biggest support system during this time. Everything and everyone had to go through her. She took charge because that's how great a woman she is. Vanessa dealt with the hospital and set up my home care. She made sure only the right people came into my hospital room and in my life. Today, Vanessa and I have the best relationship that anyone could ask for. Considering our history together and how either one of us could have reacted or responded, our relationship is a miracle. It proves to me that when you make decisions you feel are best, even when others don't understand or like them, things will eventually turn out well for everyone. Ana made sure to visit frequently. She and my good friend, Eric, gave their full and whole-hearted support.

Then the lawyers started showing up, as this incident was grave and serious. I almost died. Was I turning into a vegetable? What about my foundation? Was I even going to survive this? I eventually got my memory back, but now had to face the recovery to my severe traumatic brain injury. Leaving the hospital and going home after a month in a hospital bed was one of the hardest transitions. All this new trauma (physical, emotional, mental, and spiritual) was new, frustrating, and very dark. I was on IVs, medications, and going through some serious rehabilitation. I was completely discouraged and depressed on a daily basis. I was a broken man. Ana was my in-home nurse, all the while she was going to school and working a job. My friend, Indra, and her husband, Aaron, brought me food. Another great friend, Matt, walked with me by my side around the block and talked with me. My other good friend, Raymon, handled the critical areas in both business and my personal life that would've easily fallen apart. A great man and Young Warriors mentor, Don, took the reins with the boys for our first two years. He took charge of mentoring and gave his all, loving the kids and running the program. He is naturally great with children and has the heart of a warrior.

I couldn't get around on my own—not even to the restroom—without falling down. I wasn't able or allowed to drive or cook for myself for six months. I needed someone there to watch me 24/7. My ex-girlfriend who was at the hospital every day for a month, helped me at home daily as well. Yes, I needed help, but I missed her touch. She was giving me her attention and some much-needed TLC. We were still broken up, but over the few months of her caring for me, I realized I had fully fallen in love with her. I thought in my mind, *oh maybe she gets the importance of us now.* I had never seen this attentive side of her before. I then told her how sorry I was back then assuming she was hiding something from me and that I was working on my trust issues. I apologized for projecting that onto her. I told her I was all in moving forward. I really missed her and her affection. There we were again romantically involved.

After about a few weeks, she eventually stopped her daily visits, which was a little strange. She said she had work training and her days coming over slowly diminished. She would come by once or twice a week. My feelings of mistrust started to resurface again. I was trying to convince myself that everything was fine. She was just working hard and doing what she needed to do. Was all this true or was my brain injury messing with my mind?

Meanwhile, Vanessa took me to see the doctors, came to help me recover physically by doing yoga with me, answering emails and phone calls from friends and social media questions. Everything. I can't believe her kindness... well actually, I can. Like I have alluded to throughout this book, Vanessa is locked in as my lifetime friend and confidante!

I did come to a definite realization about relationships and a deeper understanding of the meaning of family during this time. Although I had plenty of acquaintances and supporters, I didn't realize that they are not quite the same as close or true friends. I have since learned the difference. Many friends did text or call when they first heard what had happened. But after a few weeks, much of that stopped. One of my close friends kept asking if he could help, but he didn't know what to do. The thing is, I did want help, but I didn't know what I wanted or needed at the time. I was just not well. Nobody could make the pain go away. Not family, friends, doctors, not the lawyers—nobody except God.

Even though I didn't want to talk to or see anyone for a very long time, friends still showed up. They still called and still helped. Eric would call or come see me almost every day once I came home from the hospital, just to check and see how I was doing and how I was feeling. He and David Hill, who was an ex tight end for the Rams, hosted a GoFundMe and a surprise fundraiser to help with my medical bills. And now I know why he called every single day. He was my true friend. He has been one of the greatest gifts in my life. He cared for me and was worried about me. Just like Leo did many years ago, Eric believed in me as a man when I needed it most. He believed in me when I couldn't believe in myself. I can honestly say from the bottom of my heart that Eric Dickerson has been my great friend, business partner, brother, mentor, and father figure. He's a loyal, loving, and supportive human being who truly cares. One sunny day, Ana drove me to a brain injury support group at Northridge Hospital. I noticed the name of the building I was entering and was surprised to see the name, The Carole and Harold Pump Women's Center. Were these the same Pumps that supported the Young Warrior's Foundation all these years? Lo and behold, it was. Their sons, Dana and David Pump, had been donors to our foundation. They were supporting me personally in my time of need by providing space for my recovery. You never know how far someone's generosity will go, but the possibilities are endless.

One of my other true friends, Joe Buzzello, lives in Scottsdale, Arizona. Even though he is a six-hour drive away, he came to visit and called me often. He joked that he needed to "lay eyes on me," because he didn't believe that Big Jay Hill got beat up that bad. Even though he lived in another state, he talked to me and visited more than other friends who lived only a few minutes away. Joe would call me every week to encourage me and check on me. I ended up feeling comfortable enough to tell him that I wasn't sure about life and living. I told him I felt like I was probably not going to get better or get back to my old self again. Joe is an excellent listener, and a very good man. He suggested I should wrap up this book with my current situation. What better way to finish a book designed to help people through the darkest of times than to explain how I had to survive one more test? There were a few other amazing people who were also helpful during this time.

On Father's Day weekend, a time when I was just regaining enough strength to leave the house, though still unable to drive, my ex-girlfriend arrived in her brand-new BMW to take me out. She wanted to make the weekend special for me. We planned a local staycation in Downtown Los Angeles and booked a beautiful one-bedroom condo on Airbnb. That evening, she surprised me with a dinner and a cupcake inscribed with "Be My Forever?" It felt like a proposal. Her intentions seemed clear, she was gonna be my ride or die through this long recovery process. Overwhelmed with emotion, I said of course. Knowing I wasn't alone in my long battle to recover. Holding her hands, I looked into her eyes, I expressed my feelings and readiness and commitment to spend my life with only her. It was a night of beautiful promises, an emotional high.

But just weeks later, the facade crumbled. I discovered she had never fully ended things with her ex-husband throughout our two-year relationship. In fact, while I was fighting for my life in a coma, she had recommitted to her marriage with him, accepting a new proposal including a new ring. The BMW, which I thought was a gift from her parents, was actually from her husband. I had been living a real life novela, trying to support her through what I truly believed was a divorce, similar to my own recent experience.

When confronted, her confession was a mix of guilt and justification. She admitted to lying constantly throughout our entire relationship, claiming confusion and a misguided attempt to protect me from an even deeper depression. Her heart, she said, was never fully mine, as she couldn't let go of her husband. My already wounded brain and body now had to contend with a shattered heart. This betrayal was so much more than a romantic deception; it reopened childhood traumas of abandonment and deceit, reminiscent of my mother's drug-fueled absences and a childhood of broken promises.

In the beautiful aftermath as I recovered, I realized the signs were always there, and very clear. My intuition had been screaming warnings, but I just could hear my own voice, deafened and blinded by a desperate need for love and care. This wasn't just about a cheating partner; it was a painful echo of my past, a cycle of seeking comfort in my own illusions rather than facing my reality. It was a self-inflicted wound, where emotions overpowered instinct.

This experience emphasized the importance of the tools that make us Warriors – willingness, action, and responsibility. Had I listened to my inner voice, had I been willing to confront the truth, maybe I could have spared myself this unnecessary emotional suffering. But in that moment of vulnerability, my desire for connection and care from her overshadowed everything else.

Along with this additional emotional trauma, I was left wondering if another attack was coming from that coward of a man who sucker punched me in the back of my head, adding to the layers of trauma and uncertainty. His identity was still unknown.

This chapter of my life, though excruciating, was a crucial lesson in honoring one's intuition and healing deep wounds to break free from destructive patterns. It's a testament to the journey of finding the warrior within, a journey that is essential for anyone grappling with similar traumas and betrayals.

Ana was surrounded by my negative energy, heartbreak, and depression. She was my caregiver, a college student and was working full time. She couldn't take it anymore, and nor should she have to. We eventually got into a huge argument. I yelled at her, saying that if she didn't like the rules here to get out. So, regretfully she did. When you have a brain injury, you have very little control over your emotions. I treated her like a 10-year-old girl and not the 20-year-old woman she was. She was already dealing with repressed anger and resentment toward me for the way she said I Bible-bashed her in her upbringing. I was an emotionally unstable asshole at that time. I was still very sick and just done. After Ana moved out, I ended up leaving Los Angeles and headed to Arizona. I moved in with my friend and an NFL athlete, Ricky Seals-Jones. It was nice to live with company and he is such a great guy. I was depressed and it worked for me to be alone because he was naturally a quiet person, and he would travel for work, and gone a lot.

I experienced darkness before, but this was another level of darkness I didn't know existed. It was in the dungeon of the darkest place of my soul. I just wanted things to end.

Major depression was now in full effect. I was living in a dark bedroom, uninspired to get out of bed. I couldn't have the lights on. I tried to laugh as much as I could, but all I could do was cry. I watched all nine seasons of "The Office" three or four times and then I would lay in bed crying at night. I was among the skies of misery in the darkness alone. All I had was my TV and computer. I started researching on a regular basis the most painless ways to commit suicide and how to do it without hurting others. After about four to five months of research, I had a significant plan.

Here I was in the desert where I hardly knew anyone, and I would try to heal alone. If I healed back to normal then that would be amazing and I could restart Young Warriors in Arizona, but I knew that I probably wouldn't be my old self again, so I had a Plan B. Really though, it was kind of my Plan A. If I couldn't heal, then I would end it fast in the desert. I could go die alone somewhere peacefully and just disappear from the Earth. It was another level of darkness I didn't know existed. It was the basement of the darkest place of my soul. I lost everything. My baby sister was gone, and at the time Ana wasn't able to come to Arizona to see me. I was playing the victim to all the unkind and unjust trauma that happened to me. I was done. I was tired.

You see, it takes courage to acknowledge the unfair and grotesque things that have influenced the very core of who you are. Facing it and healing from it is a practice of self-love and I had to rediscover willingness all over again. It saved my life before, but what about now?

Some days will be hard, and we will forget, but it's not okay to quit. Being relentless is another important crucial principle in the My Warrior's Way. Never give up! You will always be the victim until you do something about it. I know this now because at the time, I just wallowed in my wounds and sat and sat some more and started thinking about everything with a negative mindset instead of an optimistic perspective, like we teach in the program. I went from a confident powerful-minded inspiring leader to a shattered hurt young boy. Check out how easy it is to spiral... *No one checks on me anyway* is what I was telling myself in my head. It was a pity party for one. *I'm in the biggest battle of my life alone, I lost my house, my sister is dead, my daughter doesn't check on me, and my best little buddy, William, is now back in Ohio, and I am about to lose my foundation. The woman who I just fell in love with heartlessly drove an iron stake through my heart leaving me to die alone. I have nothing.*

Notice the voices here. Who am I listening to? Thoughts are powerful. They come in and ambush you over and over again. Thoughts are things that can turn into our being. And our being can turn into our actions. I can be the biggest bully to myself, convinced I didn't do enough in the day. I am my own worst critic. Part of me wants to beat me up. What the hell is that? I don't know if that comes from my experiences or getting railed by my mom and her boyfriends. *Don't you for real cry over that spilled milk!* Picture this, a little kid with a cup of milk trips and milk spills everywhere. "*What the hell are you doing?*" More yelling... "*Dammit!*" With rage, "*What the hell is wrong with you, you fuckin' idiot?*" That was me. I have learned to beat my own ass, mentally. Self-abuse. I have learned to be mean to me, even when there are reasons to celebrate something that went well. No matter what is going on, I tend to stay focused on what I am not doing correctly. The mistakes I have made in the past somehow have to do with the now. I am stuck in the past or stuck projecting in the future. I am either the complete best or the worst ever. I should've done more yesterday. I should've done this. I should've done that. My goodness... aren't you tired of hearing this? Changing our thoughts has the power to shift our being.

I'm either going to get through this craziness and take things to another level or I am going to quit. I'm all in either way. If I am going out, take me out. Or if I want to go big, I'm going to be the best. Eric was the first person I spoke to about having suicidal thoughts. He noticed that I was really depressed and said he was worried about me. Thank God for Eric Dickerson, I tell you. That man called me every day. Depression and suicidal thoughts are things to never be ashamed of if you are ever going through it. The damage you can do to your heart while this is going on can be intensely painful, and you will suffer. In fact, I have learned that we can create our own self-inflicted wounds when we make decisions from wounded places, and sometimes they can be irreversible and unimaginable in so many different ways. Our mental health matters. Appearance happens in two ways. The first is you can see someone's world crumbling around them, and it may be easier to detect their stress and pain. Second is the one that can catch you by surprise. There are those that look like they have it all together with their looks, money, fame, or even status, and you would never know the amount of suffering they are encountering on the inside.

When you self inflict with all the pain you are feeling, at times it can feel like you spiritually died or that you are broken. That you can't be fixed. And then you do yourself in. Really? Yeah. I thought that once. Until someone held safe space for me. We must build authentic relationships, because that is where it becomes safe to be vulnerable and express really scary things like suicide. Especially us men, regardless of whatever appearance we have. Men believed in me. And today I am by your side to tell you that I am that somebody for you. Your life matters. Isolating and hiding these feelings are never good. The National Suicide Prevention Hotline can be reached 24 hours a day (800-273-8255) or dial 988. You can also reach out to someone you know who loves you. Just don't do this alone. We aren't meant to go through life and hard times by ourselves.

I'm also convinced that we need to be more real as men. Stereotypes have screwed up a lot of people. You know what I mean? Men are silently bullied by other men to never 'sit' down or concede easily. The masculine norm is to not share feelings or discuss emotions. It is ingrained in our heads at an early age that it is not appropriate for boys and men to feel feelings or cry. Only girls do that. Don't be a bitch. Only women do that. There is no room for weakness. Man up! That is a phrase I have come to dislike. Can we deconstruct this, please? Honest, strong, and brave men share their pain with their real homies. That is a real man. I've shared a lot of crying moments spread out all through this book and it's important to know that it is okay for men to cry. Being afraid of judgment or embarrassment can keep us from being vulnerable and becoming stronger. Find a safe tribe where you can be you. I hope you can relate to what I am about to say. It takes tremendous strength and fierce courage to talk about that which is hidden and to allow the trauma to release. That, my friend, is manning up. Men, give yourself permission to trust your gut and heart, from the place that you are healed from and not from the narrative of your wounds. Think it all through. Some choices are not going to please everyone. You are not here to please others. Your authenticity and truth alone will inspire yourself and those around you.

After I lost everything, the universe sent me another little hero. You see, I became close to my ex-girlfriend's brother-in-law and his family and gained a nephew. Little Leo was three at the time. He was a young boy full of life and a mirror of who I am and why I do what I do. Leo was such a giant help, emotionally, during my many days of loneliness. Kids seem to always bring a smile to my face, especially Leo. He would FaceTime me with his cute little manly voice and tell me he loved me. But he also required me to make him laugh by saying, "Tio Jay, put on a funny mask and make funny faces." So, I would. I would pull myself out of bed, find one of my Halloween masks and do what I love to do anyway, which is make kids smile and laugh. He would laugh throughout the entire call, which in turn would make me laugh. It will always be one of my brightest moments during those dark times. He is forever one of my superheroes. His father, Kikie Sanchez, was such a great listener during this time, and became like a real brother to me. They were part of my road to recovery.

I have known all along that there is evil out there. It has stared me in the face a few times. It comes to kill, steal, and destroy; this time it came for all of me: my spirit, my body, my mind, and my heart. It fears you and me because we are set here on this Earth for the greater good. There is a saying in Mexican culture: "No me se rajar." It means I don't know how to give up. I will not crack or break, no matter what is thrown at me. My friend, Phil, reminded me of this. I loved it so much, I have it along with a picture of my daughter now tatted right below my collarbone. They both remind me that no matter what happens, I can get through it. I've done it time and time again. When I look in the mirror, what looks back at me is a daily reminder of how powerful human beings are. We are resilient and strong.

I did have Vanessa, Eric, and little Leo constantly encouraging me. Feeling better and better, I started working out. Then a little light of hope and healing began. Hope is everything. It is why poor people can happily say *I am blessed*, while a rich person may feel empty inside. I had to relearn everything. I had a new brain. Having a traumatic brain injury can stink because no one can see it or tell you specifically if things are better or how long it will take to get back to normal. In truth, there is never a new normal. Our bodies change constantly. Change is inevitable. We are ever-evolving beings. Fact is, now I have a new brain. And at this point, I must do my own processing.

The process has been painful, but it has led me to greater self-awareness. Coming out of the injury, I had no multi-tasking ability, I could only focus my attention on one thing at a time; and yes, it has improved over the years. When I walk, I am conscious of it. I have to be. This has actually served as a gift. Self-awareness is when you are conscious and knowledgeable of not only the physical part of you, but also your feelings, motives, desires, and your own character. This is the last principle in the My Warrior's Way. When you are self-aware, you have your mind's attention and that is a great thing! You will know what you have, what you need, and what others may need. I knew this about myself: I needed help and accountability. Meditation and yoga have helped tremendously. I had to hire a trainer to show me how to eat correctly again, and not just work out, but to have an exact routine every day. I was given a clear plan: how many sets, reps, and times of the day to eat. I hired an assistant to help with the program. I hired someone to clean my place. It's a whole form of rehabilitation. I asked my friend, Matt Fisher, who is a well-renowned professional golf coach, if he could help me get my golf swing back. He helped me remember that I never really had a great golf swing in the first place. We laughed. You don't need hundreds of people to heal. I have a few good people in my life and that is all I need. I also had to let go of some people who were not for me or aligned with my ambitions and values. These were minor external improvements and miracles, and I thank God for them.

Cleveland Browns Game
Jason (Right), Ricky Seals-Jones (center), Eric Dickerson (left.)

NO ME SE RAJAR!

Leo and his Tio Guerote

As I was healing and feeling better physically and mentally, I wasn't healed emotionally. I really was done and felt like screw screw screw screw it all. Life is short. I held on to all that pain since my split from the church and my divorce. This sent me back to numbing up with my familiar old ways of coping. Sometimes as a warrior, you must go into the wilderness time and time again to remember who you truly are. Tristan, in the movie, *Legends of the Fall*, left home countless times and it was painful being out there; but it was necessary for the ultimate homecoming. He never stopped being a warrior, though. You can still wander and be a warrior. You may not be in full practice, but the take-downs will give you an opportunity to come back stronger, wiser, and knowing love more than you did before. Remember, no quitting is the only hard rule of a warrior.

We can be our own worst enemy. The only one who can defeat that part of us is that other greater part of us. You always have to come back to your heart. Your heart is good. Pay attention to your thoughts: do they lead to thinking about death, or are they thoughts that speak of life? Sometimes you must slow things down and become aware of what you are thinking. Words can have major power. Especially when it comes to life and death.

What are you affirming and who are you affirming? It starts with you and a thought. Before we know it, we may spiral down the rabbit hole, having an ultimate grand finale outcome. It's frightful-future land. Most of the time it isn't even real. We live there and we spend so much energy in places that will only bring us down. You are not your thoughts, and neither am I. Our job is to observe the thoughts, see them come and go, and remain in the present moment and truth.

The foundation took a major hit because I took a major hit. Literally. The assault cost me and the foundation so much. We didn't grow in the way we had been for the last decade because I was the foundation's founder, CEO, mentor, secretary, and janitor. I did everything. Looking back, I see things differently, I was becoming a WARRIOR. A true, bonafide, heart-led warrior. The kind of person that this program needs. It also gave me the opportunity to re-learn how to trust my Creator again.

I would like you to think about some of the hardest things that have ever happened to you. Those seeds of sorrow can be your greatest transformations. God can take your wounds and make something beautiful of it. Beauty from ashes. Now I can wear it as a badge and be proud of what I have overcome. Now I have authority to speak to a broken world. My self-awareness now works to make me better, not tear me down. This is another key component to the My Warrior's Way. Self-awareness is major. How about you? I may not know how to become a doctor, an engineer, or a lawyer, but I know how to climb out of a gutter, clean myself up, and fight for myself and others. That is my gift. That is my calling. When living the My Warrior's Way principles, you can apply them to anything you desire to be... a better husband, single father, doctor, lawyer, firefighter. It doesn't matter, you now have the tools. Use them.

I even get why all of it has happened to me. No need to spend my energy asking why anymore or playing the victim. It's a miracle that I am still here. I am grateful to be here with you, sharing my story.

"We cannot become what we want by remaining what we are."

—Max De Pree

CHAPTER 9
WELCOME HOME WARRIOR

By now you may know my life has been a roller coaster of extreme ups and downs. It took me over 40 years to find my tribe. Blood relatives don't have to be your only family. With the support of my personal and professional community, and the strength I drew from their belief in me, I was able to recover, survive, and thrive. Make no mistake about it, for the most part, what I have around me and inside of me, I learned the hard way. I've had to fight like a warrior (mainly with myself) almost every step of the way to achieve the success, peace, and happiness I have had. I came into this world with two big obstacles: there was no dad in the picture and my mom was a drug addict. Things were not safe, and I didn't have a protected environment.

It seems I've been searching for approval from men and women all my life. I have always felt embraced by many different cultures, but I especially felt loved and accepted by Black and Latino cultures. My experiences felt warm as they welcomed me into their lives ever since I was a small child. I didn't feel ignored or belittled. They've invited me into their homes, fed me, and loved me. It's more than just being accepted. I felt embraced and accepted as I was, and that takes it to a different level. This is my experience for more than 25 years.

In some of the neighborhoods where I grew up, I didn't feel dismissed or bullied like I did at home or some of the schools I went to. In fact, I felt more than welcomed. The men in my house were always drunk or drugged out, and really, really abusive to my mother, and especially me and my sister. My sister and I were the little mongrels always in the way. Every single man my mom brought home ended up treating me like a piece of shit, teased me, ordered me around, and straight up made it clear they didn't like me. Even to this day, at times I feel a sense of intimidation and unworthiness around some older white males. Men that look just like me. That is what childhood trauma can do. The good news is I am conscious of it and have done the work and continue to do my own work on the origin of those beliefs. I know our country has centuries of generational hurts of White dominance and supremacy and we have a lot of responsibilities on our hands; I can say that as a White male. I just know I personally have felt my own version of being looked down upon or not accepted as I am. It is why social justice is part of the foundation's work.

In hindsight, I find it incredibly ironic that many of the people who somehow left a positive impression on me when I was a kid were those I met in my Section 8 neighborhoods. Growing up, all of us were poor together, fathers or mothers were missing, and no one really worked. I soon learned that not everyone lived like I did. As I got older, support from people of color continues, and I am grateful. I had to forgive those who hurt me and my family. I had to learn to respect and eventually trust not just my own shade, but all shades.

It is perplexing to me that some people just don't believe that all cultures can live harmoniously in any society if their minds are open. As a person who has observed and experienced lifestyles and values with a myriad of people and cultures throughout my life, I can honestly say without reservation that I have love in my heart for all of them. It's not about Black, White, Asian, Christian, Muslim, Catholic, or Jewish. We all have a heart that basically looks the same inside any human being on this planet. And I see this as the biggest gift of all: to love all cultures, including my own. For me, it's the heart of the man, not the color of his skin, that I connect with. I proclaim here today that I am grateful for every special person who has entered my life and found a place in my heart: White, Black, Brown, or Tan. I am a better person today because of you.

What I value the most is family. This isn't confined to the traditional sense but extends to the kind of love and care that a mother and father would give their children. It's a beauty I've discovered in Latino culture, where every greeting is filled with genuine warmth, kisses, and hugs, making me feel whole and loved. This is the celebrity treatment in its truest form, where I'm welcomed and cared for just as I am.

Consider how fans might treat LeBron James or Will Ferrell if they walked into their homes. The excitement, the warmth, the eagerness to make them comfortable – that's how I've been received by families like the Sanchez's and the Garcia's. My journey with Latino culture began in a Home Depot parking lot, where I first experienced their embracing and nurturing nature. But it was the Garcia family who provided the most intense and enduring Latino love for about 13 years, leaving an erasable impact on my life.

When I turned 45, Kikie and his family, the Sanchez's, surprised me with a birthday gathering at their home. It was a time when I was battling a broken heart and mind, and their home emerged as a sanctuary where I could be a broken man without judgment. During those darkest times, and especially throughout the Covid-19 pandemic, little Leo and the entire Sanchez family became my haven, offering me years of unwavering support and care.

Kikie and I shared similar experiences in our youth, and the love and safety his family offered were transformative for me. In my eyes, he became like a brother, and Leo, a nephew to me. "Amo a la mi familia Sanchez" – I love the Sanchez family. This sense of belonging was a new experience for me, one that I hadn't found even in my own home. During that time, Kikie, his wife, and their family welcomed me with open arms, providing a warmth and love that was deeply appreciated.

This experience was distinct from the love I received from the Garcia family, which was also profound and genuine. However, my connection to the Garcia's was intertwined with my marriage to Vanessa, making it a different kind of familial bond. With the Sanchez's, it was Enrique Senior who, without saying a word, recognized my pain and extended his family's care to me. This gesture was especially meaningful, considering my complicated connection to their family as the ex-boyfriend of Kikie's wife's sister. Their acceptance and support during a time when I could offer little but drama in return was a testament to their compassion and empathy.

Life is complex, and relationships evolve. Kikie and I, bound by circumstances that were always going to be challenging, have drifted apart. Our connection, formed during a time when I was recovering and vulnerable, couldn't withstand the external pressures. It's not about bitterness or anger; it's about understanding the reality of our situation. I cherish the time I spent with the Sanchez family, especially with Leo, who unknowingly filled a void in my life. His innocent love was a gift during a time when I was cut off from my own emotional and mental well-being. I tattooed a portrait of my little Leo on my thigh as a testament to this profound impact.

Enrique, Kikie's father, provided the fatherly love I had longed for all my life. It wasn't anything extraordinary, just the natural affection of a father for a son, which was enough to change the course of my life. I am grateful for you, Enrique Sr.

The Latino culture, with its ethos of working hard and loving your family fiercely, resonates deeply with me. This is evident not just in my personal relationships but also in my Young Warriors program, where most participants are Latino. The mutual love and appreciation we share is a testament to the culture's profound impact on my life.

As I move forward, I carry with me the love and lessons from these years. The bond with Leo and Enrique, the nurturing embrace of the Garcia family, and the countless moments of Latino love and support remain cherished parts of my journey, reminding me that blessings often come intertwined with pain. And while the future of my relationship with Kikie is uncertain, the gratitude for what his family and the broader Latino community have given me will always be a part of who I am

Guerote and Enrique

Eric Dickerson and his family in Los Angeles and in Houston have become my family also. His cousin, Buffy, and her family are down to earth, hospitable, loving, and welcome me with open arms every time. They care about me.

The boys and families in our program are my family. I have found the missing pieces of my life in the lives of the boys, young adults, and men who embrace our desire to help them. There are so many fatherless Latinos and African Americans in the Los Angeles area. It truly amazed me when I first started the program. Honestly, the way that first group of boys showed their love and appreciation for what we were trying to achieve was humbling. They needed us and I needed them. It has been so very encouraging to my soul. My love for them is on another level of family, and that's why I consider all Young Warriors—all my boys and their families – my family. Straight up true love and respect. They warm up my heart so much and reward me more than I can describe. Young Warriors is part of my tribe.

OK. Let's do this, think of your favorite sports team or band. A group of people that you would be so grateful to spend time with for just a few hours, even if it's one time. Who would that be? People actually pay lots of money to experience being around Hall of Famers, A-Listers, musicians, and a host of other fan favorites. For me, I would have paid all the money in the world for a safe, loving, protecting and supportive family, mother and father. God just so happened to choose to place me in the world of Hall of Fame athletes, who became my friends, my mentors, my supporters, and my family. It's a hubling life experience and I'm grateful to have them in my life. But you know what? As much as people desire and crave to hang with the fame and the fortune in the high class lifestyle, my joy is enjoying sitting with one of my Mexican familes in a backyard or on a patio watching them be all about each other and talk shit at the same time, I love it. Picture a Superbowl party. Something like that. It feels that good to me! That's how I feel about being part of a humble, loving families with a serving and giving hearts. God is funny with us sometimes because He knows the whole story. We just know up until this moment. He knows the end of your story too, so don't stop now. He gave me so many things I desired; just not how I pictured it. For instance, I get those same celebrity feelings from the kids all over Los Angeles. I love those kids and families, and they love me.

I remember one time when I was terribly ill from eating at the Mercado in Jiquilpan, Michoacán, Mexico, Enrique took care of me like a father would. He brought me to the emergency room and even gave me a paleta (popsicle). I felt like a real son. I was in my early 40's and I felt like I was 10. It was an amazing feeling. I was a loved son. It was one of my favorite times I've been sick.

I'm grateful for all of it. Sometimes you must endure tremendous pain to get tremendous blessings.

Beautiful souls from these cultures gave me true love and a belonging. Isn't that really what we are all searching for? They gave me the identity of love. I've been searching for an identity for over 40 years. I've questioned it throughout my entire life. WHO AM I? I could never seem to answer that for myself. I found my identity in Love, and it will stay rooted in LOVE. A divine love that cannot be taken from me. I love myself and I love who I am.

I constantly laugh at myself. I know I'm an anomaly; I have come to accept that I am different than you. I'm unique, and so are you. Own it. Live it and you'll see. I don't know who my legitimate, biological father is, so now I can play with the possibilities. I have no idea what his name is, race, nationality, or skin tone; nothing. I don't know if he is big or small. Kind- hearted or mean. Stupid or smart. And I often wonder... is he funny like me? Is the man even alive or is he dead? And then I smile and just have fun with it, like many areas in my life of tragedy and challenging times. This is the path God chose for me, and right now I am having the time of my life.

In Los Angeles and Mexico, where I have woven deep connections with my Latino friends and family, I am fondly known as Guerote. Pronounced 'whe-roe-tay', this nickname is a derivative of 'Guero', a term commonly used in these regions for light-skinned Mexicans and white people. It's a term of endearment, not of offense. I stand tall and big, so 'Guerote' – adding 'te' for emphasis – distinguishes me, the Big Blond White Guy, from others.

Interestingly, Guerote has evolved into more than just a playful nickname; it represents my embraced identity, distinct from the ego-driven persona I often found myself trapped in. Previously, I was caught up in a whirlwind of ego, insecurity, and fear, constantly worrying about others' perceptions. I remember the discomfort I felt growing up, being teased for embracing different cultural traits. Society often tries to confine our thoughts, leading us to judge and be judged.

However, Guerote symbolizes my transformation. It signifies the love and acceptance I've found within the Latino community – a community that has welcomed me at various stages of my life. It's a badge of my heart's restoration and a new identity. Whether interacting with Latinos for the first time in a Home Depot parking lot or mingling with diverse social groups, I've felt an unwavering acceptance, an acknowledgment of my true self beyond superficial labels.

Guerote is not about adopting a Mexican identity; it's about the identity of love that I've experienced through the Mexican people. It represents gratitude, respect, reverence, honor, and most importantly, love. This term embodies the unconditional love I've received and my desire to reciprocate it. It's a testament to the power of acceptance and love in transcending cultural and linguistic barriers.

My journey as Guerote has been one of gratitude and appreciation, far removed from any notion of pity or dominance. It's a journey of a man, Jason, who is silly, funny, confident, and grateful. It's about acknowledging my roots while celebrating the rich tapestry of relationships that have shaped me. Guerote is a reminder that love and acceptance are gifts, and in embracing others for who they are, we find our true selves. And it does not come from a place of pity or dominance from a White man over minorities or anyone else, but from a real solid place of gratitude and appreciation. It's respect. It's reverence. It's honor. Most importantly, it's love.

When you find a connection with your identity through your roles, status, looks, or abilities, that can be dangerous. Why? Because it can all be taken away. Then what? Mine was stripped before I was born. Do you know how much of my life has been spent dwelling on the fact that I am without a dad... a fatherless child, a wannabe, abandoned, and not good enough? The person who made me isn't here. The role of that person was to develop me, but that didn't happen. For me, that translated to having to prove to women, family, friends, and the world that I was somebody. I tried doing it in different forms, but all from my ego. Not good! Back then, my ego was a bully, and along with the rest of society, shaped my identity. But let's get something straight. I have learned that we don't earn our identity or develop it with our own strength. We are never doing this alone; it's all given to us by our Creator. There is nothing I need to do to have it. There is nothing to prove. Being God's child alone is enough. I am enough. I am all that He has created me to be.

As the program culminates, a significant moment awaits each boy – the bestowal of a unique nickname. This ceremony is not just a formal conclusion of their eight-week journey; it's a pivotal point in their personal transformation. Each nickname, carefully chosen, mirrors their individual strengths, traits, and the journey they have embarked upon. These names become symbols of their newfound identity, tokens of empowerment, and reminders of their intrinsic worth.

This practice of assigning nicknames has a profound impact. It instills a newfound confidence and a sense of pride within these boys – a feeling many of them have never experienced before. It's a moment that often marks the beginning of a new chapter in their lives, where they step into a world with a stronger sense of self and a heart full of courage.

Through this tradition, we channel the lessons learned from my own traumas and triumphs. It's a testament to the journey of turning one's painful experiences into a source of strength and inspiration. My journey through life, marked by overcoming challenges and finding my identity, now serves as a beacon for these young souls. It's about showing them that their past does not define them, but rather, it can empower them.

In essence, what we offer these boys is more than just a nickname – it's a key to unlocking the confidence and self-belief that lies within them. It's a way of saying, "You are seen, you are valued, and you have a unique place in this world." This practice is a powerful affirmation, a declaration that they, too, can overcome their struggles and emerge stronger.

Through this initiative, I live out my passion – to prevent others from enduring the hardships I faced. It's a journey of healing, not just for myself but for every boy who steps into our program. We're not just creating warriors; we're nurturing heart-led leaders of tomorrow, each with a unique story and a powerful, meaningful name to carry forth.

John Eldridge has a great quote:

"*Identity is not something that falls on us out of the sky. For better or for worse, identity is bestowed.*"

—John Eldredge & Brent Curtis

YOU ARE UNIQUE. OWN IT

The universe was like, "Jason, you are loved. Embrace it!" When Jesus came, he didn't behave and look like everyone else. He talked differently and was hugely misunderstood. You know what's crazy about some people not getting me? Guess who didn't get Jesus? His own people! That is true. The Jews did not like the Jew. His own people could not accept Him, so they rejected Him and killed him. As tragic as this was, His example gives me hope and excitement in being authentically me. I am finally in a place where I have fully accepted who Jason Hill really is. I am grateful, regardless; some people die never knowing who they really are. What I mean by this is, not where you are from or what your ethnicity is, but who you are as a person and human being. What you love, what you dislike, what makes you smile, what hurts you... that is who you are. This is why I love *Guerote* so much. It is a reminder. I am a whole man. I am accepted for who I am. *Guerote,* my strong spirit, has reminded me that I am valuable, good enough, and true to myself and others. *Guerote* is an indicator of who I am, especially when hardship and darkness come.

I want to tell you why I feel so strongly about my name, *Guerote.* God gives names. He gave Abram a new name: Abraham; and Sarai was changed to Sarah. He called Jacob—Israel. These names were given to them after they reached a higher state of thinking and living. They, too, got their names because they went through the darkness before they saw the light. It is common with Gurus, spiritual teachers, and those unattached in marriage to change their names to honor a milestone or accomplishment. Bestowed names are repeated in social settings. When addressed as such, these names mean more than our given name because within that name is a purpose accomplished or a battle won. Those knighted with new names remember their meaning. They remember their purpose and what it took to get them there.

When I am spiraling or feeling unaligned, I remember that *Guerote* is who I am, my birthright, and my blessing. I am a whole man. A powerful man. Most importantly, a loved man. Most of all, it brings me back when I am lost. He is my higher self. A spiritual piece of me. God knew who I was when He designed me. It has taken most of my life to finally understand this, and I am grateful for every bit of it. God allows things to happen in order to heal us, strengthen us, deconstruct us, and fully initiate us, like a homecoming. It is the return to your heart. It is the call to return home, and it takes a true warrior to get there.

Remember Simba in the movie, *Lion King*? He was in the wilderness figuring out who he was, and it was only when he saw the reflection of his father in the water did he get it. When I looked in the water, there was no reflection of my father. I was a lost boy. However, at the end of the day, I am a child of God, and the reflection I see now is His reflection. Simba is called to remember who he is. *"Remember."* It is then when he returns to his kingdom to defeat his evil uncle, Scar, to reclaim the throne that has always belonged to him. I believe we all need to go through this process of initiation. It is as if someone is knighting, crowning, or anointing you, and you receive a new name. It is an identity being bestowed. When our Young Warrior boys are bestowed, they know they will go on their journey, make mistakes, and encounter battles of all shapes and sizes, but they are equipped to be who they are intended to be.

Don't get it twisted. You will encounter the haters and critics. So, what? They will be there when you are succeeding and when you aren't. So why not do what you love and be who you really are? Go BE you. Let everyone see the real you, it is such a freeing feeling. Everyone sees the real me. Sometimes it's like living in a glass house because the living is out loud. All that matters to me is caring about the broken boys and men who will see themselves climb out of the gutter, heal, and champion on. Sure, at times we make poor decisions, but I will continue to choose to live a life of sacrifice. Learn from my mistakes and love from my heart. A caring man. Not perfect. I don't have it all figured out and that is okay. It's important to enjoy it all. Enjoy life and all it has to offer.

There's always something positive and beautiful on the other side if you can get through it, which I believe you can. Now it's your turn. Go be yourself in life, even if it's hard or embarrassing for others. Your authenticity may bring out their personal insecurities and judgments on themselves. Don't judge them either, just as you didn't want them to judge you. You may free them from living a lie, too. Just keep being yourself, making people laugh, making people feel loved, and making people feel better than they did before you walked into their lives. That's all you can do, my friend. If you do that, I believe with all my heart and all my experience that the Universe and God will provide you with your *why* in this life and you can fulfill not only your dream, but His dream for you.

My favorite sports teams are all the Cleveland teams. I grew up so passionate about sports and especially my Ohio teams. I looked up to these incredible athletes, bought their jerseys and sports cards. I watched all the games as a kid and still do. I love every part of it. I imagined what it would be like to meet them one day and even dreamt of being a professional athlete. I lived down the street from LeBron James when I lived in Eastland Woods but at the time, he was just a young kid.

It's hard for me alone to believe that these amazing athletes and Hall of Famers support the foundation, like Kenny Lofton, Bernie Kosar, and Eric Metcalf. Hall of Fame running back Jim Brown of the Cleveland

Browns became a friend. How did this happen? I will tell you... God. This is what it looks like when you trust your heart and Him. The impossible happens. All I wanted growing up was a loving family, good friends, and people I could trust with my pains and mistakes to help me become a stable and balanced man. All kids and adults want to be loved, accepted, and adored, and now I feel blown away at how it all came about. Remember my roommate, Ricky Seals-Jones? In 2019, he was signed by the Cleveland Browns and there I was—on the field in my home stadium at a Browns game! What in the world?! After the game, I found myself having dinner with Eric, Jim Brown, and the Cleveland Browns' owners, Dee and Jimmy Haslam. Honestly, it's a trip how the universe gives you everything you need and what you desire. I'm just thankful.

Find your tribe: pick five. Allow a small circle into your life to mastermind with and lift each other up. You are safe to share your weaknesses with your homies. To overcome battles, you will need your tribe. No one can make it alone, not even the strongest warrior of them all. True meekness is strength under control, and it's calling on your brothers when you need to. You will face many wars in this lifetime and each battle prepares you for the next great one. Are you ready? Evolve and learn from every challenge. They will only make you greater. The warrior is inside of you, waiting to bust out.

Yes, through the years I have questioned how different my life may have been if my father was involved or if my mother was more stable and balanced. I thought for sure that I may have become a pro athlete. Maybe in the NFL. I am 6'2" and weigh 225 lbs. Most of my friends are NFL players. I know this. God hasn't made any mistakes and all of these circumstances have been part of my battle and triumph. Young Warriors would have never been created without His plan for me, and for that I am grateful.

I still have a long journey ahead of me, but I recognize the huge mountains I've already conquered, so the mountains in my future don't seem very big; not anymore. I do not believe God hurts people. I would never hurt my child to teach her a lesson. I do believe that karma exists. I also believe God will take our bad karma, poor choices, our pain, and our struggles and help us through it with His love and grace. Then we win, and so does He. In sports, it's all about the win. So as tough as things have been in my life, and as hard as things currently are right now, I truly believe that there is always a win coming for me—and for you.

Let me be clear here. I know right now I am struggling. I am struggling to believe everything will be okay. As a matter of fact, as I write this, I was diagnosed with two brain aneurysms. Is this related to my brain injury that happened when I got sucker punched? It is very possible. Sometimes, I wonder how all this happened, and I have to wrap my mind around how to live this new life. Is it really a matter of coming down to what is fair or unfair? I already told you, life isn't fair for anyone, but does that mean you stop giving your gifts and love away? No, it doesn't. I am a kind-hearted, emotionally available, generous, and caring man. That is who I am and that is who I will continue to be, regardless of the challenges I face. The man who caused my brain injury and almost killed me in 2017 is now out and roaming free. A year after the incident, he was identified and arrested. The prosecutors charged him with a felony assault with a deadly weapon, and five years in prison. At that court date, the prosecutors consulted me on the sentencing details as they do with all victims. I didn't know this man and he didn't know me. We were strangers. All I kept thinking about were my own past mistakes and having compassion on this man. What if I would've gotten caught for some of the things I did? I made horrible decisions out of emotion. I understood those mistakes. I told the prosecutor, "Do as little as you can," and explained why, so they did a plea agreement. That was six months in jail and probation for the next five years. If he violated probation within the five years, he would have to go back to prison for the full term. I felt like I was offering him a gift by letting him off the hook. He almost took my life, and here I am living with these physical problems for the rest of my life. Looking back, this man wasn't ready to receive the grace and the compassion that I offered, because a year after that in a civil deposition, he lied about everything. And that hurt. I now know not everyone is ready to receive the gifts your genuine heart wants to offer, and that is okay. Should I have forgiven this man for all of it? Yes. Forgiving him was a gift to myself, a crucial step in ensuring I don't revert to the bitterness and resentment that once defined me. This conscious act of forgiveness is vital for my own wellbeing, allowing me to move forward as a whole man, fully aware and accepting of who I am. Being true to myself is paramount, far outweighing the allure of harboring bitterness and resentment. Living with such negativity is a path I refuse to tread. My journey from being a young man with a problematic attitude—'a big dude, don't fuck with me' kind of mindset— to becoming the solution now, underscores the importance of mastering my emotions and anger. It's about taking control, doing the hard work to reach a place of genuine forgiveness, because I know all too well how resentment can transform me from being part of the solution back into a significant problem. Both versions of myself hold immense power, but it's through forgiveness and truly confronting my feelings that I harness this power for positive change. Living with resentment is something I'm not interested in doing. He is on his journey, and I am on mine. God only knows the outcome.

Truth is, many days over the last several years getting myself out of bed was the hardest task of my day but I continued to show up even in that moment. Get up, move, stay in motion. My good friend, Eric, tells me, "Patience my brotha. Patience." I have been here several times. At the moment, it's important for me to remember this truth. Although I know it's hard, I am with you and get it. No matter what great hero or movie you love, it's always the worst parts of that movie or hero that make the end amazing. It's up to us to not stop watching the movie before it's over. That is what I almost did. It felt like my movie was over, but it wasn't... and it isn't. I am alive and in living color.

When I started writing this book, my primary goal was to help others overcome whatever it was that they were going through. I felt I had gone through so much in my past that I had a tremendous amount of wisdom and experience to share with you, who may also be going through significant challenges. And I certainly did. Then that random act of violence the night I was celebrating a friend's birthday and the new young warrior inductees shifted everything. For the first time in many, many years, I had to heal by fighting a battle I was, yet again, not prepared for. I also had to make sense of why this horrific thing happened to me. On top of all this, COVID showed up we had to deal a new way of life and a new set of rules. It has been devastating for the foundation, but I've been here before. Remember, there's no quitting for us. You see, a warrior is a being who trains all the time and is prepared for any feat and challenge when those times come.

There were so many things that occurred in my past, things that were so painful and challenging when I was a boy, a teenager, and then a young adult. And over time, I went back to the distractions and still continue to learn and grow. But why this? And why now? The only thought that made sense to me was that God wanted me to experience something more and become an even stronger version of myself. And to

FIND YOUR TRIBE!

remind me that life includes both good and bad. I've moved past a lot of tough times, and I'll probably experience more tough times in the future. Of that, I am sure. I just gotta stay humble, hope for great outcomes, and live my best life every single day. The best life for me means a life of service. I get to sit with those who are hurting and listen to them. Whether it be friends, family, or those in the program, and we also have a lot of good times, too, laughing and having fun. When I am able to also do this with my daughter, it is the best because she is the sweetest and so much fun to be with.

So, I'm writing this almost six years after sustaining injuries that left me in a coma, unable to think or walk straight. And this book has become something different than I originally intended. Instead of trying to simply help others overcome things that were challenging during their youth or in their past, I am now writing from a perspective of the present. I've had to take my own medicine and figure out how to survive some very dark days over the better part of the last few years. I've been down and out before. I've been very sad, even hospitalized for clinical depression. But never have I ever had to overcome as much pain and suffering that I have endured over these last few years. These moments really felt like the end and now I know it was part of my journey. I've spent my life discovering what it takes to become a Warrior. Living MY WARRIOR'S WAY has saved me and others. And so now I share it with you.

As a warrior, you start off young. Attacks on the heart begin early. The heart is wounded and vulnerable and over time it can harden with all the future hits and heartbreaks it will encounter. I believe the heart will continue to break until it breaks wide open and brings you to your knees. And even after that, another great battle awaits. But guess what? Once you do the work and are healed, you are stronger, wiser, and more equipped. What's a life if it's not really lived to the fullest? I want you to live your true life, just as Maximus in the movie *Gladiator* and William Wallace in the movie *Braveheart*, like a true warrior who is willing to take major losses, hurt, and feel pain for the battle of humanity. Warriors have a cause. They face and conquer evil. They train and learn how to defeat darkness with an inner and outer discipline. There is a way of the heart that when the warrior awakens, he also learns how to love, protect, rescue, and become a service to beauty. There are so many things a warrior must accomplish and learn from. I feel like I am in the final stages of living between warrior and the beginning stages of a king. Many of my friends are referred to as being a G.O.A.T. (**G**reatest **O**f **A**ll **T**ime). They earned that.

One great mentor of mine, along with Eric, is NFL Coach, Anthony Lynn. What a heart this man has, I tell you. Aside from the amazing work he does coaching young men in the NFL, he makes a tremendous effort mentoring members of the community with his organization called the Lynn Family Foundation. He came to one of our golf tournaments a few years back and made it a point to tell me that he, too, was a fatherless kid. That day, he met some of our boys in the program and took the time to talk with them. Things evolved and Coach Lynn and I just became closer through the years. I tell him all the time I still need mentoring. I've learned so much from this man. He is dedicated, disciplined, and organized. He's up early cracking away and the man is always working. He really is the best at what he does, and the most important thing is that he knows it. Not in an arrogant way. He learned from others in his life and has put all of it into practice. There is no reason for him not to believe he is the best in the league. He knows it. One day I asked him why he didn't come across as cocky, even though he was very self-assured.

*Eric Dickerson (left), Jim Brown, Jason Hill, Eric Metcalf, and
Bernie Kosar (right).*

Young Warriors fundraiser at Townhall in Cleveland Ohio

Jason (left), Isabelle, Anthony Lynn, Rafael, and Aaron (right). Lynn Family Foundation and the Young Warriors Foundation partnered to support a family in Jalisco, Mexico, with housing, furniture, TVs, bedroom sets and basic essentials, along with lots of love.

Jason Hill (One of the many childhood homes)
Cuyahoga Falls, Ohio

His response was, "I just believe that I am great, and I work hard to believe that. Someone has to be the best. Why not me?" It was cool to hear him say it, mean it, and believe it. We should all know how incredible we are. I want to own that and believe that about myself. I want to learn from his example and realize how hard I worked at not quitting.

Men like Coach Lynn and the GOATs in my life mentor and inspire me to be my best and help others to be their best, as well. I will always need that mentoring in my life.

Kings are the fathers around me: my mentors. My goal is to be a G.O.A.T. but first I need to become a king. A king uses his influence for the sake of others: To serve and protect his people. I want to accept that mindset and know deep in my being that I am at my best when I am working with fatherless boys and any hurting man or child. What does that mean? That means I have confidence in my work to heal and love these kids as if they were my own. That is what I am the best at doing. I understand their pain and suffering. I take everything given to me by my amazing mentors and pass the torch to the young ones I work with. We want these boys to know how to become a GOAT themselves one day. I am here, I am all in, and I love every minute of it. I want to wake up every morning knowing that I am spending my life serving and helping others heal. By example, I wish to help others feel the same way I do. Wounded healers healing the world. Imagine that.

I've come to realize how much the wilderness and darkness can be the biggest blessings of our lives. But what is it that really sends us there? For me, it was being hurt and let's just say it... feeling pain. Fear scares you. Pain changes you. With un-dealt pain and grief, if not conscious, I tended to turn to the two places I always knew: sex and alcohol. It is good to have moderation. I've been through some unimaginable experiences, just as you probably have. But when I look at my life today, I'm overwhelmed with gratitude. For me, at this time in my life, gratitude is not just a feeling; it is a choice.

Going through this dark time taught me one last, but very valuable lesson; one that I want to pass on to you before I wrap up this book. I've realized that I want to be great at being there for those in need, even more than I already have. I want to be the best at being there for the people close to me who I love and care for. I also want to be there for people who are hurting, afraid, and injured. It's important to know that even if people tell you they don't want to see you or talk to you, I believe they want to know they are loved. That's the lesson. Everybody wants to feel loved.

Do that for people. Help them feel loved. Love is not just a feeling, it's also an action. You've got to start it to feel it. If you know someone is hurting but they say they want to be alone, be respectful of that; but also show them some love. Maybe you show up at their home with a folding chair. Sit in their driveway and text them a selfie. Let them know you are there because you want to be. Tell them they don't need to text you back. Just stay awhile so they will know somebody really *does* love them. Do whatever you have to do to make that person feel loved. All human beings, especially in these times, need to feel loved and understood.

Live your life like a warrior. Do this for yourself and do it for others. All the attention on my recovery opened up my own ability to experience self-awareness.

I will always remember one thing Vanessa told me during my recovery. After waking up from my coma, she asked me who my favorite sports team was. Without missing a beat, I replied, "The Cleveland Browns, of course." And that's when she knew I would make it through this, that even with the brain injury and my physical trauma, I was still in there. This attack—and one of my worst years—coincided with the Browns' worst season ever. They lost every single game they played, and usually by a lot. That's right: 0 -16. After trading their quarterback and drafting a new one, they saw a complete turnaround in 2018. And I did, too, starting to really recover from my traumatic brain injury in a way that is rare. Me and the Browns will continue to improve! In 2020, after twenty plus years, the Browns made the playoffs, and for the first time in my life, thanks to my friend and Young Warrior supporter, Stan Ross, I went to a Cleveland Browns playoff game. As the Browns continue to get better, so will I. *Make it happen, Cleveland Browns! Make it happen, Jason Hill! Guerote's got you!*

Live from your heart. Live with all you've got. Recognize your warrior heart and conquer whatever is in front of you. Stay present.

The world needs you. You are writing your own story. Don't stop and definitely don't quit. Live your warrior's way. Be **W**illing. Be **A**ctive. Be **R**elentless. Be **R**esourceful. Be **I**nspired. Be **O**ptimistic. Be **R**esponsible. And always be **S**elf-aware. It's about BEING them and DOING them. Your adventure toward happiness, self-love, freedom, and victory awaits. If you hang in there, I'm telling you that it will be one hell of an adventure and a battle worth fighting for.

Go for it, my friend... **Activate your WARRIOR spirit. Start fighting from your heart. Forgive and heal. Be and Live Your Warrior's Way!**

EPILOGUE

Wow! What a journey! Thank you for reading my book, going on this wild ride with me and taking in the details of my struggles. I hope in some way you have been inspired. Maybe you were thinking about changing but didn't know where to start or who to turn to. You know, I don't know you, but I'll say it again, I care for you and your journey. I mean that, friend. Please don't quit. You got this. Trust the process! Sure, I had to face some unfortunate tragedies, but being able to break free physically, emotionally, and mentally are miracles and gifts. I also had to do my own inner work, forgive, and heal. I wouldn't have been able to achieve these victories had I quit all those times I wanted to give up. I wouldn't trade these lessons learned for the world. I had to dig deep and become something else instead of a broken being.

Okay, so yes, I didn't have a father and I still don't know who or where the man is, but am I supposed to let that define and ruin my chances at being great and extraordinary? Does his absence and my mother's drug use have to be the reason I stay small, shrink back, and stay afraid of making any moves in this life? That was a hard answer. I had to reinvent who I was and give myself a new identity. *Guerote es lo que soy!* If I stuck to my old story, I would've ended up dead, on the streets, or in prison, like many of my friends and family. I had to remove myself from the toxic environments, fight for my daughter, forgive in my heart, and change my perspective.

Serving and caring for others has given me freedom to no longer be a lifelong victim. No more victim here. Sure, I am now a CEO/Founder, writer, mentor, and speaker; but more importantly, I am a WARRIOR and still developing that. There is so much more I want to do and am committed to do for humanity. I am a heart-led Warrior. You are becoming one, too. You just may not see that yet. You will if you stick to your WARRIOR'S WAY. Trust me. I have dedicated my life to helping people who are hurting and can't seem to find a way out. I hope this book has been a safe place for you, especially for all the things you are healing from. For me, I had to make a plan and build a process. That is what evolved into what I now call the My Warrior's Way. It's called my because it is unique to you. Your journey is not mine, and mine is not yours. It is your way. Your path. But we are all Warriors.

The My Warrior's Way came from my own process in the battle of discovering my identity and my wholeness as a man and a human being. I'm finally comfortable and secure with who I am. I have become comfortable with others being uncomfortable with me. I am not like you, and I'm not supposed to be. And you are not like me. I am me in all my unique and extraordinary ways; and I have a message that I believe helps the world, and I believe the same about you. And that is what makes us one and the same.

I faced extremely dark times but looking back, this process not only saved my life, but it also became the method I use when I get lost or overwhelmed, and it's the curriculum used today for the kids in our program and for adults who are hurting. It's a universal teaching of becoming and living with purpose, no matter who you are or where you are. If you are fighting a disease... if you have a giant goal that you want to achieve.... struggling with the damage you've done to yourself or others...

living on the streets... quitting smoking... trying to pass your high school classes... trying to accept yourself, you will benefit with this proven process.

Before you close this book, I would like to quickly break down the W.A.R.R.I.O.R.S. acronym now to tell you how I did it. There's so much more to this, and it's really amazing, but here's the heart of it:

I had to be **WILLING** to do the things I didn't want to do. I had to take **ACTION**. I took personal **RESPONSIBILITY** for the things I did. Forget about what others did to me. I had to start with myself first. The choices I made as a kid, father, husband, friend, employee... I was able to see my mistakes and take responsibility in those areas. I had to be responsible in forgiving others. I'm still learning how to be a better friend, father, worker, best friend, leader, and role model. I had to become **RESOURCEFUL** and use the many resources that became available to me. In doing so, I had to stay humble and continue to be humble; the ego is always wanting to be our imposter. I used resources and grew in a lot of areas. I had to stay **INSPIRED** in my dark days and find inspiration through friends, music, movies, and especially by the few who I could trust when I was vulnerable. My personal challenges have always been believing that I was no good. It was self-abuse, really. It was sad to see what I had done to myself through my own self-talk and choices... all because of my unhealed childhood wounds. In reality, I have learned this about myself: I am a really good man who had to overcome so many things. I had to be **OPTIMISTIC**. I had to choose to see the glass half full; and I added a little more optimism to the cup, then added a little more.

I really had to push hard through my brain injury, which stripped me of everything I had, including my ego. It has taken me more than five years to heal. I found myself more focused and **RELENTLESS** in overcoming my physical and emotional pain, especially as I got older. I had some great resources, friends, and a wonderful support system. Sometimes that is how you have to be: vulnerable with your hurts, and relentless in your pursuit of happiness. There was no quitting. It's never going to be perfect; in fact, it can be messy; but no quitting allowed. **SELF-AWARENESS** is huge. Commit and do the work. It's not easy and it's not free. Real sacrifice comes with a cost, and every tear you shed will be worth it. So worth it.

Now it's your turn, Warrior. The My Warrior's Way process is something you can go back to in any area of your life... time and time again. It's a mindset and a warrior's way of living. You can always go back to this process and re-group. We are always working on ourselves and loving ourselves through everything. I know you can do it, and I'm behind you all the way. I'm here with you in spirit. You are not alone, even when you are by yourself. If you hang in there and Warrior up, the pain and suffering will heal and reveal your trueness. You will see the beauty in that. They were always there to help you grow. There is so much to learn. The universe knew you could handle it, overcome, and identify with those who might be going through similar things. The world, your friends, and family need you.

Thank you to the beautiful country of El Salvador for hosting me, especially to the children in the town of Suchitoto for awakening my life's purpose and providing the Young Warriors Foundation vision. Thank you to every single person who helped me become the Heart-Led Warrior that I am today. I am eternally grateful.

Ana Mackenzie Hill... I love you.

—Jason Robert Hill

"You have power over your mind – not outside events.
Realize this, and you will find strength."

—Marcus Aurelius

"*A warrior feeds his body well; he trains it; works on it. Where he lacks knowledge, he studies. But above all he must believe. He must believe in his strength of will, of purpose, of heart and soul.*"

—David Gemmell

YOUNG WARRIORS' PHILOSOPHY

B efore we part, I would like to tell you about the My Warrior's Way that will assist you in living the life of a **W.A.R.R.I.O.R.** These are the principles we use to select mentees, mentors, and staff in our **Young Warriors** program. To know more about the Young Warriors Foundation or to get involved, go to YoungWarriors.org

These key philosophies help us establish the mindsets and attitudes for the participants and the entire organization. The key to our success comes from the environment we create inside the walls of each school and community site we work with. We like to break down our overall philosophy into these principles, all of which create a combined result in transformation from a lonely, insecure human being—whether male, female or however you identify to a strong, confident **Warrior!** Let this be your personal and daily practice.

I WILL BE:

1. WILLING

A desire to pursue and fight for positive change in my life.

2. ACTIVE

Making my desires happen by taking definite action.

3. RELENTLESS

Sticking to your Warrior Way. No quitting!

4. RESOURCEFUL

Identifying and using the tools I need to be my best.

5. INSPIRED

Find it, use it and offer it.

6. OPTIMISTIC

Having a positive outlook about the direction of my life.

7. RESPONSIBLE

The constant battle of duty over my thoughts and actions.

8. SELF-AWARE

Conscious knowledge of my character, thoughts, motives and actions!

REFERENCES

Beattie, Melody. (1992). *Codependent No More: How to Stop Controlling Others and Start Caring for Yourself.* Hazelden Publishing.

Brown, Brené. (2010). *The Gifts of Imperfection: Let Go of Who You Think You're Supposed to Be and Embrace Who You Are.* Hazelden Publishing,

Dweck, Carol. (2016). *Mindset: The New Psychology of Success. How We Can Learn to Fulfill Our Potential.* Random House Books.

van der Kolk, Bessel. (2014). *The Body Keeps the Score: Brain, Mind, and Body in the Healing of Trauma.* Penguin Books.

RECOMMENDED RESOURCES

Wild at Heart by John Eldredge

The Way of The Wild Heart by John Eldredge

Fathered By God by John Eldredge

Strengths-Based Leadership by Tom Rath and Barry Conchie

Why Are All The Black Kids Sitting Together In The Cafeteria? By Beverly Daniel Tatum, PhD

The Anger Workbook by Les Carter, PhD, & Frank Minirth, MD

The Holy Bible

Father Fiction by Donald Miller

The Cap Equation by Joe Buzzello

The 7 Habits of Highly Effective People by Stephen R. Covey

The Mentor Leader by Tony Dungy

Crucial Conversations by Kerry Patterson

In The Realm of Hungry Ghosts by Gabor Mate

Do The Work by Steven Pressfield

Tribes by Seth Godin

The Four Agreements by Don Miguel Ruiz

You Owe You by Eric Thomas, PhD

Non-Negotiable: Ten Years Incarcerated − Creating the Unbreakable Mindset by Wes Watson

YOUNG WARRIORS' FOUNDATION

Inspiring Fatherless Boys to Become Great Men

Mission: Inspiring boys to become great men.

Vision: We envision a world full of confident, balanced, and stable men making positive contributions to society.

LEARN MORE ABOUT YOUNG WARRIORS

YoungWarriors.org
@YoungWarriorsLA

GIVE TODAY

Jason 'Guerote' Hill

Jason 'Guerote' Hill is available for speaking at your event, coaching and teambuilding workshops. Reach out to book Jason for an event.

BOOK JASON

Guerote.com
@Guerote

Becoming a Warrior

BecomingAWarrior.com

BUY THE BOOK

Made in the USA
Middletown, DE
22 February 2024

49710672R00135